A–Z of Microwave Cookery

Carol Bowen is a freelance home economist and cookery writer. She has contributed to the national press and magazines, broadcast on radio, acted as consultant to manufacturers of food and kitchenware, done photographic styling for advertising and books and worked as cookery consultant for TV-AM's *X-Cel Diet* with Diana Dors. Her other cookery books include *The Microwave Cookbook* and *The Food Processor Cookbook*, also published by Pan, and *Versatile Vegetables* (Octopus) which won the 1984 Bejam Cookery Book of the Year Award. Carol Bowen is married and lives with her husband and children in Surrey.

Other cookery books available in Pan

Carol Bowen

A–Z
of Microwave
Cookery

Pan Original
Pan Books London and Sydney

First published 1987 by Pan Books Ltd
2nd edition published 1987 by Pan Books Ltd
Cavaye Place, London SW10 9PG
9 8 7 6 5 4 3 2 1
© Carol Bowen 1987
ISBN 0 330 30360 0

Photoset by Rowland Phototypesetting Ltd
Bury St Edmunds, Suffolk
Printed in Great Britain by
Richard Clay Ltd, Bungay, Suffolk

Foreword

It is often said that the simplest ideas are the best – and the idea for this book, very simple though it may seem, arose from countless requests for basic microwave information at demonstrations, during radio phone-ins and from readers' letters gathered over the last few years. It seemed from discussions with microwave owners that it was extremely easy to find out from the multitude of glossy microwave cookbooks around today how to cook something as special as *coq au vin*, but hard to find a guide which gave times for cooking basic everyday foods. The information was undoubtedly to be found in the glossies, but the mound of information that had to be waded through first was overwhelming and far too time-costly if all you wanted to cook, for example, was a few baked tomatoes to go with a mid-week grill.

The result of such requests was therefore to produce a quick at-a-glance A–Z guide for cooking and thawing, if appropriate, basic foods as different as apples and yoghurt. And here it is – the culmination of many years' research work, testing and recipe development, involving over 200 foods that are suitable for cooking the microwave way.

Each food item, listed in alphabetical order, has brief, but precise, instructions for preparation, arrangement, covering, turning or stirring and standing times to give excellent results, alongside cooking times according to weight and power level used. Already this handy guide has proved an indispensable aid in my own kitchen and rarely strays from its well-earned place on top of the microwave. I hope it will find a privileged place near yours.

Carol Bowen

Acknowledgements

I should like to offer my grateful thanks to Sharp Electronics (UK) and Philips Electronics for kindly supplying the ovens on which all testing was done for this book.

Special thanks also go to Gail Ashton for typing the entries, to nanny Elizabeth Kempton without whose help this book would never have been compiled, and to my husband Peter for his never-decreasing enthusiasm for my projects.

Before You Begin

- All the timings in this book have been tested using ovens with a maximum output of 650–700 watts. The ovens also had variable power and the descriptions used refer to the following power outputs:

  100% (High) = 650–700 watts
  70% (Medium/High) = 500–550 watts
  50% (Medium) = 300–350 watts
  30% (Low) = 200 watts
  20% (Defrost) = 150 watts

  The chart overleaf gives approximate power outputs in watts at these levels and their relative cooking times.

- The microwave ovens used for testing also had a turntable facility. If yours does not, then follow the basic rules given in your microwave handbook for turning, rearranging and rotating foods at regular intervals during the cooking times.
- Metric measurements may vary from one entry to another within the book and it is essential to follow either metric or imperial.
- Note that unless otherwise stated, flour is of the plain variety, water is cold, eggs are size 3, sugar is granulated and all spoon quantities are measured level.
- Government guidelines now recommend that cling film with plasticisers, i.e. pvc film should not be used as a covering or lining for foods cooked in the microwave. All cling film referred to in this book is of the 'polythene' film kind without plasticisers and can be found under such brand names as Purecling, Saran wrap and Glad wrap. This type of film does not cling as well as standard pvc film, but can often be more manageable when pulling back to stir during microwave cooking. If you do not wish to use cling film as a covering then use an upturned plate, saucer, special microwave plate cover or baking parchment instead.

GUIDE TO COMPARATIVE MICROWAVE OVEN CONTROL SETTINGS

Descriptions of settings used in this book	20% (Defrost)	30% (Low)		50% (Medium)		70% (Medium/High)	100% (High)
Descriptions of settings available on popular microwave ovens	1 keep warm low 2	2 simmer 3	3 stew medium/low 4	4 defrost medium 5	5 bake medium 6	6 roast high 7–8	7 full/high normal 10
Approximate % power input	20%	30%	40%	50%	60%	70%	100%
Approximate power output in watts	150W	200W	250W	300–350W	400W	500–550W	650–700W
Cooking time in minutes (for times greater than 10 minutes simply add the figures in the appropriate columns)	4	3¼	2½	2	1¾	1¼	1
	8	6¾	5	4	3¼	2¾	2
	12	10	7½	6	5	4	3
	16	13¼	10	8	6¾	5¼	4
	20	16¾	12½	10	8¼	6¾	5
	24	20	15	12	10	8	6
	28	23¼	17½	14	12	9¼	7
	32	26¾	20	16	13¼	10¾	8
	36	30	22½	18	15	12	9
	40	33¾	25	20	16½	13¼	10

Glossary of Terms Used

BACON RACK   A special rack designed for use in the microwave that is non-metallic and raises the bacon above its own juices during cooking for crisp results.

BROWNING AGENT   A home-made or commercially prepared mix used to give food (especially meat) the colour of conventionally cooked food. Popular ways of browning include brushing with soy sauce, Worcestershire sauce, a barbecue sauce, tomato ketchup, sprinkling with ground paprika or basting with dark molasses.

BROWNING DISH   A dish made of a glass ceramic substance with a special coating that absorbs microwave energy. After preheating, food is added and the dish duplicates the conventional browning and searing processes of conventional cooking. Always follow manufacturer's instructions for use.

COVER/COVER LOOSELY   Cover food tightly or loosely with either a lid, cling film, greaseproof paper or absorbent kitchen towel.

DISH/BOWL, ETC.   Use dishes, bowls and containers that are microwave safe, i.e. non-metallic. Do not use plastics that are not considered dishwasher safe, waxed cartons, melamine or lead crystal.

LEAVE TO STAND Leave the food or dish untouched for the time specified, often covered, to make best use of residual heat in the food.

PREHEAT Usually refers to preheating of a browning dish. Always follow manufacturer's instructions – although most recommend a preheating time of 5 minutes at 100% (High).

PRICK OR PIERCE Prick or pierce foods with the prongs of a fork, the tip of a knife or a cocktail stick to release pressure or prevent pressure building up during cooking.

REARRANGE Rearrange items of food from the edge of the dish to the centre and vice versa, half-way through the cooking time, unless otherwise stated.

ROASTING RACK/RACK A special rack designed for use in the microwave that is non-metallic and raises roasts and baked items above the base of the dish during cooking, reheating or defrosting, for good results.

ROTATE Give the dish or food a quarter or half turn half-way through the cooking time, unless otherwise stated.

SCISSOR-SNIP Cut the fat with scissors at regular intervals to prevent curling during cooking.

SHIELD Protect sensitive and vulnerable parts of the food by covering with small pieces of foil for about half the recommended cooking time, unless otherwise stated.

STIR Stir the food half-way through the cooking time, unless otherwise stated. Stir from the outside of the dish to the inside to distribute heat evenly.

TO THAW AND REHEAT	Times and instructions are given here for thawing and reheating the food in *one* operation.	
TURN/TURN OVER	Turn the food over half-way through the cooking time, unless instructions specify more regular turning.	
VENTED CLING FILM	Cover with cling film that has either been pierced with a few holes or rolled back slightly at one corner to allow steam to escape and to prevent a ballooning effect.	

ROASTING CHART USING A MICROWAVE THERMOMETER

Meat	Remove from oven when this temperature is reached	After standing, meat will reach this temperature for serving
Beef: rare	55°C/130°F	65°C/150°F
medium	60°C/140°F	70°C/160°F
well done	70°C/160°F	78°C/170°F
Pot roasts	65°C/150°F	70°C/160°F
Meatloaf	55°C/130°F	60°C/140°F
Veal	65°C/150°F	75°C/165°F
Lamb	70°C/160°F	82°C/180°F
Pork	75°C/165°F	85°C/185°F

A

ADUKI BEANS
ALMONDS
APPLES
APPLE SAUCE
APRICOTS
ARTICHOKES
ASPARAGUS
ASPIC JELLY
AUBERGINES

Aduki Beans

TO COOK SOAKED BEANS: Place soaked beans in a cooking dish. Cover with boiling water. Cover and cook for the first time and power setting. Reduce the power setting and cook for the second time, adding extra boiling water to cover if needed. Drain to use as required.

Quantity	1st Time/Power	2nd Time/Power
225g/8oz	10 minutes/ 100% (High)	10–15 minutes/ 50% (Medium)

Almonds

TO BLANCH: Pour water over almonds and cook, uncovered, for time specified. Drain and remove skins. Leave to dry on absorbent kitchen towel.

Quantity	Water	Power	Minutes
100g/4oz	250ml/8fl oz	100% (High)	1

TO BROWN: Place almonds on a large flat dish. Cook for time specified, stirring once every minute. Allow to cool.

Quantity	Power	Minutes
25–50g/1–2oz whole	100% (High)	5–6
25–50g/1–2oz flaked	100% (High)	3–5

Apples

POACHED IN LIGHT SYRUP: Peel, core and slice apples and place in a cooking dish with 300ml/½ pint hot sugar-syrup. Cover loosely and cook for the time specified, stirring once. Leave to stand, covered, for 5 minutes. Serve hot or cold.

Quantity	Power	Minutes
450g/1lb	100% (High)	3
900g/2lb	100% (High)	5–6

STEWED: Peel, core and slice apples and place in a cooking dish with sugar. Cover loosely and cook for the time specified, stirring once. Serve hot or cold.

Quantity	Sugar	Power	Minutes
450g/1lb	100g/4oz	100% (High)	6–8

BAKED: Wash and remove the cores from the apples and, using a sharp knife, score a cut around the middle of each to prevent bursting. Place in a cooking dish and add a little sugar, dried fruit and butter to each if preferred. Pour water around fruit and cook for time specified, rearranging once.

Quantity	Water	Power	Minutes
4 large	8 tbsp	100% (High)	9–10

FROZEN DRY-PACK APPLE SLICES: Place in a dish, cover and cook for the time specified, stirring once. Leave to stand, covered, for 5 minutes before using.

Quantity	Power	Minutes
450g/1lb	100% (High)	4–8

FROZEN SYRUP-SOAKED AND PACKED APPLE SLICES: Place in a dish, cover and cook for the time specified, stirring once. Leave to stand, covered, for 5 minutes before using.

Quantity	Power	Minutes
450g/1lb	100% (High)	8–12

FROZEN FREE-FLOW APPLE SLICES: Place in a dish, cover and cook for the time specified, stirring once. Leave to stand, covered, for 5 minutes before using.

Quantity	Power	Minutes
225g/8oz	20% (Defrost)	3–4
450g/1lb	20% (Defrost)	8

FROZEN APPLE PURÉE: Place in a dish, cover and cook for the time specified, breaking up and stirring 2–3 times. Leave to stand, covered, for 5 minutes before using.

Quantity	Power	Minutes
300ml/½ pint	20% (Defrost)	5–7
600ml/1 pint	20% (Defrost)	10–12

Apple Sauce

Place peeled, cored and sliced apples in a bowl with water, sugar, a knob of butter and a dash of lemon juice. Cover and cook for the time specified, stirring once. Beat until smooth, leave chunky or purée in a blender to serve.

Quantity	Water	Sugar	Power	Minutes
450g/1lb	1 tbsp	2–3 tsp	100% (High)	6–8

Apricots

TO PEEL FRESH: Place water in a bowl and cook for the time specified. Add the apricots and leave to stand for 1–2½ minutes to loosen the skins. Remove with a slotted spoon and immerse in cold water – the skins will now peel away easily.

Quantity	Water	Power	Minutes
6–8	750ml/1¼ pints	100% (High)	9–10

TO PURÉE FRESH: Place stoned but not peeled apricots in a cooking dish. Cover loosely and cook for the time specified, stirring once. Leave to stand, covered, for 3 minutes then purée in a blender or pass through a fine nylon sieve.

Quantity	Power	Minutes
450g/1lb	100% (High)	4–5

(to make 300ml/½ pint purée)

POACHED IN LIGHT SYRUP: Skin, halve and stone, slicing if preferred. Place in a cooking dish with 300ml/½ pint hot sugar-syrup. Cover loosely and cook for the time specified, stirring once. Leave to stand, covered, for 5 minutes. Serve hot or cold.

Quantity	Power	Minutes
6–8	100% (High)	3–4

TO STEW FRESH: Stone and wash apricots. Place in a cooking dish, sprinkle with the sugar, cover and cook for time specified, stirring once. Leave to stand, covered, for 5 minutes before serving.

Quantity	Sugar	Power	Minutes
6–8	100g/4oz	100% (High)	6–8

FROZEN HALVES: Place in a dish, cover and cook for time specified, separating once. Leave to stand, covered, for 10–15 minutes before using.

Quantity	Power	Minutes
225g/8oz	20% (Defrost)	4–5
450g/1lb	20% (Defrost)	7–9

FROZEN HALVES IN SYRUP: Place in a dish, cover and cook for time specified, breaking up and stirring twice. Leave to stand, covered, for 10 minutes before using.

Quantity	Power	Minutes
225g/8oz	20% (Defrost)	10–12
450g/1lb	20% (Defrost)	13–15

Artichokes

GLOBE: Discard the tough, outer leaves. Snip the tips off the remaining leaves and trim the stems to the base. Wash and shake to remove excess water. Stand upright in a cooking dish. Pour over water (or stock) and lemon juice. Cover and cook for the time specified, basting and rearranging twice. Test if cooked at the minimum time by pulling a leaf from the base; if it comes away freely the artichoke is cooked. Leave to stand, covered, for 5 minutes before serving.

Quantity	Water	Lemon Juice	Power	Minutes
1	6 tbsp	1½ tsp	100% (High)	5–6
2	8 tbsp	1 tbsp	100% (High)	10–11
4	150ml/¼ pint	2 tbsp	100% (High)	15–18

JERUSALEM: Peel and cut into even-sized pieces. Place in a cooking dish with the water or butter. Cover and cook for the time specified, stirring once. Leave to stand, covered, for 3 minutes before serving.

Quantity	Water	or	Butter	Power	Minutes
450g/1lb	4 tbsp		25g/1oz	100% (High)	8–10

Asparagus

FRESH WHOLE SPEARS: Prepare and arrange in a large shallow dish with pointed tips to the centre. Add water, cover and cook for the time specified, rearranging spears but still keeping tips to centre half-way through the cooking time.

Quantity	Water	Power	Minutes
450g/1lb	125ml/4½fl oz	100% (High)	12–14

FRESH CUT SPEARS: Prepare and place in a large shallow dish. Add water, cover and cook for time specified, stirring once.

Quantity	Water	Power	Minutes
450g/1lb	125ml/4½fl oz	100% (High)	9–11

FROZEN WHOLE SPEARS: Place in a cooking dish with water. Cover and cook for time specified, rearranging once. Leave to stand for 5 minutes before serving.

Quantity	Water	Power	Minutes
450g/1lb	125ml/4½fl oz	100% (High)	9–12

CANNED WHOLE SPEARS: Drain and place in a cooking dish. Cover and cook for time specified, rearranging once.

Quantity	Power	Minutes
1×425g/15oz can	100% (High)	3–4

CANNED CUT SPEARS: Drain and place in a cooking dish. Cover and cook for time specified, rearranging once.

Quantity	Power	Minutes
1×300g/11oz can	100% (High)	2–2½

Aspic Jelly

FROM ASPIC POWDER: Place cold water in a measuring jug and cook for the time specified, or until boiling. Add aspic jelly powder and stir briskly to dissolve. Allow to cool before using.

Quantity	Water	Power	Minutes
1×24g/1oz packet	500ml/17fl oz	100% (High)	5–6

Aubergines

FRESH CUBES: Cut unpeeled aubergine into 2cm/¾ inch cubes. Place in a cooking dish with butter. Cover and cook for time specified, stirring every 3 minutes. Leave to stand, covered, for 4 minutes. Season after cooking.

Quantity	Butter	Power	Minutes
450g/1lb	25g/1oz	100% (High)	7–10

FRESH WHOLE: Peel off stalks, rinse and dry. Brush with a little oil and prick. Place on absorbent kitchen towel and cook for time specified, turning once. Leave to stand for 4 minutes. Scoop out flesh and use as required.

Quantity	Power	Minutes
1×225g/8oz	100% (High)	3–4
2×225g/8oz	100% (High)	4–6

FROZEN SLICES: Place in a shallow dish. Cover and cook for time specified, stirring 2–3 times. Drain and pat dry to use.

Quantity	Power	Minutes
225g/8oz	20% (Defrost)	7
450g/1lb	20% (Defrost)	10–13

B

BABY'S BOTTLE
BABY'S FOOD
BACON
BAKED BEANS
BANANAS
BARLEY
BEANS
BÉARNAISE SAUCE
BEEF
BEETROOT
BISCUITS
BLACK BEANS
BLACKBERRIES
BLACKCURRANTS
BLACKEYE BEANS
BLANCHING VEGETABLES
BREAD
BREADCRUMBS
BROAD BEANS
BROCCOLI
BRUSSELS SPROUTS
BUCKWHEAT
BULGHUR
BUTTER
BUTTER OR LIMA BEANS

Baby's Bottle

TO REHEAT READY-MADE CHILLED BABY'S MILK TO DRINKING TEMPERA-
TURE: Remove teat from bottle and heat milk for the time specified.
Shake well to distribute the heat and check temperature by shaking a
few drops onto the back of your hand before feeding.

Quantity	Power	Minutes
75ml/3fl oz	100% (High)	¼–½
150ml/5fl oz	100% (High)	½–¾
200ml/7fl oz	100% (High)	1

Baby's Food

TO THAW AND HEAT FROZEN HOME-MADE CUBES OF PURÉE: Place in a
small bowl then in the microwave with a small glass of water. Cook
until melted and thawed, stirring to break up once. Check the
temperature before serving.

Quantity	Power	Minutes
1 cube (2 tbls)	100% (High)	½–¾
2 cubes (50ml/2fl oz)	100% (High)	1–1¼
4 cubes (120ml/4fl oz)	100% (High)	1½–2

TO REHEAT CANNED: Remove metal cap from jar or spoon contents of
can into a small dish. Cover and cook for the time and power
specified, stirring once. Check the temperature before serving.

Quantity	Power	Minutes
113g/4oz jar or small can	50% (Medium)	½–1

Bacon

TO COOK BACK AND STREAKY RASHERS: Place small quantities between
sheets of absorbent kitchen towel, larger quantities on a plate or
bacon rack covered with absorbent kitchen towel. Cook for the time
specified, turning over once.

Quantity	Power	Minutes
4 rashers	100% (High)	3½–4
450g/1lb	100% (High)	12–14

READY-COOKED BACON JOINT: Remove any skin from the ready-cooked bacon joint and score the fat into a diamond pattern. Sprinkle with a little brown sugar and stud with cloves if preferred. Place in a shallow dish and cook, uncovered, for the time specified, turning and rotating once. Leave to stand, covered loosely with foil, for 5–10 minutes before serving.

Quantity	Power	Minutes
1×450g/1lb vacuum-packed joint	100% (High)	4–5

TO COOK BACON JOINT: Remove any skin and score the fat into a diamond pattern. Sprinkle with a little brown sugar and stud with cloves if preferred. Place on a roasting rack or in a shallow dish and cook for the time specified, rotating the dish twice. Leave to stand, covered with foil, for 10–15 minutes before serving.

Quantity	Power	Minutes
1×900g/2lb joint	100% (High)	20–24

FROZEN BACON RASHERS: To defrost, place packet on a plate. Cook for the time specified, turning over once.

Quantity	Power	Minutes
1×225g/8oz vacuum pack	20% (Defrost)	2–3

FROZEN JOINT: If in vacuum pack, pierce the pack and place on a plate. Cook for the time specified, turning over twice. Leave to stand, covered, for 20–30 minutes before using.

Quantity	Power	Minutes
1×450g/1lb	20% (Defrost)	8
900g/2lb joint	20% (Defrost)	15–17

Baked Beans

TO COOK BAKED BEANS IN TOMATO SAUCE, CURRIED BEANS, CASSOULET BEANS, CHILLI BEANS, BEANS IN SWEET AND SOUR SAUCE AND BARBECUE BEANS: Place in a bowl, cover and cook for the time specified, stirring once.

Quantity	Power	Minutes
1×142g/5oz can	100% (High)	1¼–1½
1×220g/7¾oz can	100% (High)	1½–2
1×447g/15¾oz can	100% (High)	2½–3

Bananas

TO BAKE: Peel and halve the bananas lengthwise. Place in a cooking dish with a little sugar and fruit juice. Cook for the time specified, stirring or rearranging twice.

Quantity	Power	Minutes
2 large	100% (High)	3–4

Barley

POT BARLEY: Toast if preferred. Place in a large cooking dish with boiling water and salt. Cover loosely with a lid or vented cling film and cook for first time and power setting. Reduce power setting and cook for second time specified, stirring 3 times. Leave to stand, covered, for 5–10 minutes before serving. Fluff with a fork to separate the grains to serve.

Quantity	Water	Salt	1st Time/Power	2nd Time/Power
175g/6oz	1 litre/1¾ pints	1 tsp	3 minutes/ 100% (High)	40 minutes/ 50% (Medium)

Beans

FRESH GREEN: Place whole or cut beans in a bowl with the water. Cover and cook for the time specified, stirring once. Leave to stand, covered, for 2–3 minutes before serving.

Quantity	Water	Power	Minutes
225g/8oz whole	2 tbsp	100% (High)	8–10
450g/1lb whole	2 tbsp	100% (High)	15–18
225g/8oz cut	2 tbsp	100% (High)	7–9
450g/1lb cut	2 tbsp	100% (High)	12–15

FRESH BABY GREEN WHOLE OR FRENCH WHOLE: Place in a bowl with the water. Cover and cook for the time specified, stirring 3 times. Leave to stand, covered, for 2–3 minutes before serving.

Quantity	Water	Power	Minutes
225g/8oz	2 tbsp	100% (High)	7–9
450g/1lb	2 tbsp	100% (High)	12–15

FRESH SLICED RUNNER BEANS: Place in a bowl with the water. Cover and cook for the time specified, stirring 3–4 times. Leave to stand, covered, for 2–3 minutes before serving.

Quantity	Water	Power	Minutes
225g/8oz	2 tbsp	100% (High)	7–9
450g/1lb	2 tbsp	100% (High)	12–15

FRESH SHELLED BROAD BEANS: Place in a bowl with the water. Cover and cook for the time specified, stirring once. Leave to stand, covered, for 2–3 minutes before serving.

Quantity	Water	Power	Minutes
225g/8oz	5 tbsp	100% (High)	5–7
450g/1lb	100ml/4fl oz	100% (High)	6–10

FROZEN GREEN BEANS: Place in a bowl with the water. Cover and cook for the time specified, stirring once. Leave to stand, covered, for 2–3 minutes before serving.

Quantity	Water	Power	Minutes
225g/8oz whole	2 tbsp	100% (High)	9–10
450g/1lb whole	4 tbsp	100% (High)	14–15
225g/8oz cut	2 tbsp	100% (High)	6–7
450g/1lb cut	4 tbsp	100% (High)	10–12

FROZEN BABY GREEN WHOLE OR FRENCH WHOLE: Place in a bowl with the water. Cover and cook for the time specified, stirring 3 times. Leave to stand, covered, for 2–3 minutes before serving.

Quantity	Water	Power	Minutes
225g/8oz	2 tbsp	100% (High)	8–9
450g/1lb	4 tbsp	100% (High)	13–15

FROZEN SLICED RUNNER BEANS: Place in a bowl with the water. Cover and cook for the time specified, stirring twice. Leave to stand, covered, for 2–3 minutes before serving.

Quantity	Water	Power	Minutes
225g/8oz	2 tbsp	100% (High)	6–7
450g/1lb	4 tbsp	100% (High)	10–12

FROZEN SHELLED BROAD BEANS: Place in a bowl with the water. Cover and cook for the time specified, stirring twice. Leave to stand, covered, for 2–3 minutes before serving.

Quantity	Water	Power	Minutes
225g/8oz	4 tbsp	100% (High)	6–7
450g/1lb	100ml/4fl oz	100% (High)	10–11

CANNED GREEN AND BROAD BEANS: Drain all but liquid specified. Place in a cooking dish with the liquid, cover and cook for time specified, stirring once.

Quantity	Liquid	Power	Minutes
1×280g/10oz can whole green	2 tbsp	100% (High)	2–3
2×280g/10oz can whole green	2 tbsp	100% (High)	4–5
1×280g/10oz can cut green	2 tbsp	100% (High)	2–3
2×280g/10oz can cut green	2 tbsp	100% (High)	4–4½
1×280g/10oz can broad	2 tbsp	100% (High)	2
2×280g/10oz can broad	2 tbsp	100% (High)	3

See also Baked Beans (page 18)
Dried Beans (page 51)

Béarnaise Sauce _____

Place the butter in a jug and cook for time specified. Place egg yolks, grated onion, tarragon vinegar and white wine in a blender. Turn on to highest setting and add the hot butter in a steady stream, blending until the sauce is creamy and thickened. Serve at once.

Butter	Egg Yolks	Onion	Vinegar	Wine	Power	Minutes
100g/4oz	4	1 tsp	1 tsp	1 tsp	100% (High)	1–1½

Beef _____

TO ROAST JOINT: Place joing, fat-side down, on a roasting rack or on an upturned saucer in a dish. Place in a roasting bag and tie loosely. Calculate the cooking time according to joint type and size and cook for first time and power specified. Reduce power setting and cook for second time and power specified, turning over once. Cover with foil and leave to stand for 20 minutes before serving.

Type	Total Cooking Time (for calculation)		1st Time/Power	2nd Time/Power
Forerib or back rib (on the bone)	Rare:	7–8 mins per 450g/1lb	5 minutes/ 100% (High)	remaining time/ 50% (Medium)
	Medium:	13–14 mins per 450g/1lb	5 minutes/ 100% (High)	remaining time/ 50% (Medium)
	Well Done:	15 mins per 450g/1lb	5 minutes/ 100% (High)	remaining time/ 50% (Medium)
Forerib or back rib (boned and rolled)	Rare:	11–12 mins per 450g/1lb	5 minutes/ 100% (High)	remaining time/ 50% (Medium)
	Medium:	13–14 mins per 450g/1lb	5 minutes/ 100% (High)	remaining time/ 50% (Medium)
	Well Done:	15–16 mins per 450g/1lb	5 minutes/ 100% (High)	remaining time/ 50% (Medium)
Sirloin or topside (boned and rolled)	Rare:	8–9 mins per 450g/1lb	5 minutes/ 100% (High)	remaining time/ 50% (Medium)
	Medium:	11–12 mins per 450g/1lb	5 minutes/ 100% (High)	remaining time/ 50% (Medium)
	Well Done:	15–16 mins per 450g/1lb	5 minutes/ 100% (High)	remaining time/ 50% (Medium)

TO COOK MINCED BEEF: Place in a dish, cover and cook for the time specified, breaking up and stirring twice.

Quantity	Power	Minutes
450g/1lb	100% (High)	10–12

FROZEN UNCOOKED BEEF JOINT: To thaw, place the beef joint on a roasting rack in a dish and cook for the time calculated below, turning over once. Leave to stand, covered, for 30–45 minutes before using.

Quantity	Total Cooking Time	Power
Joints on bone	5–6 minutes per 450g/1lb	20% (Defrost)
Boneless joints	10 minutes per 450g/1lb	20% (Defrost)

FROZEN MINCED BEEF: To thaw, place beef in a bowl and cook for the time specified, breaking up twice during the cooking time. Leave to stand for 5–10 minutes before using.

Quantity	Power	Minutes
225g/8oz	20% (Defrost)	5
450g/1lb	20% (Defrost)	9–10
900g/2lb	20% (Defrost)	17–18

FROZEN STEWING OR BRAISING STEAK CUBES: To thaw, place in a shallow dish and cook for the time specified, stirring twice. Leave to stand 5–10 minutes before using.

Quantity	Power	Minutes
225g/8oz	20% (Defrost)	5–7
450g/1lb	20% (Defrost)	8–10

See also Steaks (page 137)
       Hamburgers (page 77)
       Pot Roast (page 117)

Beetroot

FRESH: Wash the beetroot and pierce the skin with a fork but do not peel. Place in a shallow dish with the water, cover loosely and cook for the time specified, rearranging twice. Leave to stand, covered, for 5 minutes before removing skins to serve or use.

Quantity	Water	Power	Minutes
4 medium	3–4 tbsp	100% (High)	14–16

CANNED OR PICKLED: Place in a bowl, cover and cook for the time and power specified, stirring once.

Quantity	Power	Minutes
450g/1lb sliced, diced or grated	100% (High)	2–3

Biscuits

FROZEN: To thaw, arrange around the edge of a plate. Cook for the time specified, turning over once. Leave to stand for 5 minutes before serving.

Quantity	Power	Minutes
225g/8oz	20% (Defrost)	1–1½

Black Beans

TO COOK SOAKED BEANS: Place soaked beans in a cooking dish. Cover with boiling water. Cover and cook for the first time and power specified. Reduce the power setting and cook for the second time specified, adding extra boiling water to cover if needed. Drain to use as required.

Quantity	1st Time/Power	2nd Time/Power
225g/8oz	10 minutes/ 100% (High)	20–25 minutes/ 50% (Medium)

Blackberries

POACHED IN LIGHT SYRUP: Hull and rinse. Place in a cooking dish with 300ml/½ pint hot sugar-syrup. Cover loosely and cook for the time specified, stirring once. Leave to stand, covered, for 5 minutes. Serve hot or cold.

Quantity	Power	Minutes
450g/1lb	100% (High)	2

FROZEN: To thaw, place in a dish and cook for the time specified, stirring once to loosen and rearrange.

Quantity	Power	Minutes
225g/8oz	20% (Defrost)	3–5

Blackcurrants

FRESH: Top and tail and place in a cooking dish with the sugar and water. Cover loosely and cook for the time specified, stirring once. Leave to stand for 5 minutes before serving.

Quantity	Sugar	Water	Power	Minutes
450g/1lb	100g/4oz	2 tbsp	100% (High)	5

FROZEN: Place in a cooking dish with the sugar and water. Cover loosely and cook for the time specified, stirring once. Leave to stand for 5 minutes before serving.

Quantity	Sugar	Water	Power	Minutes
450g/1lb	100g/4oz	2 tbsp	100% (High)	4–6

Blackeye Beans

TO COOK SOAKED BEANS: Place soaked beans in a cooking dish. Cover with boiling water. Cover and cook for the first time and power specified. Reduce the power setting and cook for the second time specified, adding extra boiling water if needed. Drain to use as required.

Quantity	1st Time/Power	2nd Time/Power
225g/8 oz	10 minutes/ 100% (High)	10–15 minutes/ 50% (Medium)

Blanching Vegetables

BLANCHING VEGETABLES FOR THE FREEZER: Place prepared vegetables in boil-in-the-bags or heavy-duty freezer bags. Add the water, seal loosely with string or an elastic band and cook for the time specified. Plunge immediately into ice-cold water. Seal firmly, dry, label and freeze.

Vegetable		Water	Power	Minutes
Asparagus	450g/1lb	3 tbsp	100% (High)	3–4
Beans	450g/1lb	6 tbsp	100% (High)	5–6
Broccoli	450g/1lb	6 tbsp	100% (High)	5–6
Brussels sprouts	450g/1lb	6 tbsp	100% (High)	5–6
Cabbage, shredded	450g/1lb	3 tbsp	100% (High)	4–4½
Carrots, sliced	450g/1lb	3 tbsp	100% (High)	3–4
whole	450g/1lb	3 tbsp	100% (High)	6–7
Cauliflower florets	450g/1lb	6 tbsp	100% (High)	4½–5
Corn on the cob	4	3 tbsp	100% (High)	5–6
Courgettes, sliced	450g/1lb	3 tbsp	100% (High)	3–3½
Leeks, sliced	450g/1lb	3 tbsp	100% (High)	5–6
Marrow, sliced or cubed	450g/1lb	3 tbsp	100% (High)	4–4½
Onions, quartered	4 medium	6 tbsp	100% (High)	4–4½

Vegetable		Water	Power	Minutes
Parsnips, cubed	450g/1lb	3 tbsp	100% (High)	3–4
Peas	450g/1lb	3 tbsp	100% (High)	4–4½
	1kg/2lb	3 tbsp	100% (High)	6–7
Spinach	450g/1lb	—	100% (High)	3–3½
Turnips, cubed	450g/1lb	3 tbsp	100% (High)	3–4

Bread

TO COOK BASIC WHITE OR WHOLEMEAL: Mix 1 teaspoon sugar with 1 teaspoon dried yeast and 150ml/¼ pint warm water in a jug. Leave until frothy, about 10–15 minutes. Sift 450g/1lb plain white or plain wholemeal flour with ½ teaspoon salt into a bowl. Cook at 100% (High) for ½ minute to warm. Rub in 40g/1½oz butter for white bread and 15g/½oz butter for wholemeal bread. Add the yeast liquid and 150ml/¼ pint warm water, and mix to a pliable dough. Knead on a lightly floured surface until smooth and elastic, about 5 minutes. Prove the dough until doubled in size (see Proving Dough, page 114). Knead again for 2–3 minutes, shape and place in a 900g/2lb loaf dish. Prove again until doubled in size. Lightly brush with oil and sprinkle with nuts, seeds or bran. Cook for the time specified, giving the dish a half-turn 3 times. Leave to stand for 5 minutes before turning out to cool. Brown under a preheated hot grill if preferred.

Quantity	Power	Minutes
1×900g/2lb loaf	100% (High)	6

FROZEN LARGE WHITE OR BROWN SLICED OR UNCUT LOAF: To thaw, loosen wrapper but do not remove. Cook for the time specified. Leave to stand for 5 minutes before slicing or removing ready-cut slices. Leave a further 10 minutes before serving.

Quantity	Power	Minutes
1×800g/1¾lb	20% (Defrost)	4

FROZEN INDIVIDUAL BREAD SLICES AND ROLLS: To thaw, wrap loosely in absorbent kitchen towel and cook for the time specified. Leave to stand for 2 minutes before serving.

Quantity	Power	Minutes
1 slice/1 roll	20% (Defrost)	¼–½
2 slices/2 rolls	20% (Defrost)	½–1
4 slices/4 rolls	20% (Defrost)	1½–2

FROZEN PITTA BREAD: To thaw, place on a double-thickness piece of absorbent kitchen towel and cook for the time specified, turning once.

Quantity	Power	Minutes
2	20% (Defrost)	1½–2
4	20% (Defrost)	2–3

FROZEN CRUMPETS: To thaw and reheat, place on a double-thickness sheet of absorbent kitchen towel and cook for the time specified, turning once.

Quantity	Power	Minutes
2	100% (High)	½–¾
4	100% (High)	1–1½

Breadcrumbs

TO MAKE DRIED: Place bread on a plate and cook for time specified, checking constantly to prevent over-browning. Leave until cold, hard and dry and crumble or blend in a processor.

Quantity	Power	Minutes
1 slice	100% (High)	2–3

Broad Beans

TO COOK SOAKED BEANS: Place soaked beans in a cooking dish. Cover with boiling water. Cover and cook for the first time and power specified. Reduce the power setting and cook for the second time specified, adding extra boiling water to cover if needed. Drain to use as required.

Quantity	1st Time/Power	2nd Time/Power
225g/8oz	10 minutes/ 100% (High)	20–25 minutes/ 50% (Medium)

Broccoli

FRESH SPEARS: Place spears in a large shallow dish with tender heads to centre of dish. Add water, cover with a lid or vented cling film. Cook for time specified, rotating dish once. Leave to stand, covered, for 2–4 minutes before serving.

Quantity	Water	Power	Minutes
225g/8oz	4 tbsp	100% (High)	4–5
450g/1lb	4 tbsp	100% (High)	8–9

FRESH PIECES: Cut into 2.5cm/1 inch pieces. Place in a large dish. Add water, cover and cook for time specified, stirring once. Leave to stand, covered, for 3–5 minutes before serving.

Quantity	Water	Power	Minutes
225g/8oz	4 tbsp	100% (High)	4½–5
450g/1lb	4 tbsp	100% (High)	8½–9½

FROZEN SPEARS: Place in a cooking dish with water. Cover and cook for time specified, stirring once. Leave to stand for 2–3 minutes before serving.

Quantity	Water	Power	Minutes
1×250g/9oz packet	4 tbsp	100% (High)	7–8
2×250g/9oz packets	4 tbsp	100% (High)	14–15

Brussels Sprouts

FRESH: Remove outer leaves, trim and cross-cut base. Place in a cooking dish with the water. Cover and cook for the time specified, stirring once. Leave to stand, covered, for 3–5 minutes before serving.

Quantity	Water	Power	Minutes
450g/1lb	4 tbsp	100% (High)	6–7
900g/2lb	8 tbsp	100% (High)	12–14

FROZEN: Place in a cooking dish with the water. Cover and cook for the time specified, stirring once. Leave to stand, covered, for 3–5 minutes before serving.

Quantity	Water	Power	Minutes
450g/1lb	2 tbsp	100% (High)	10–11
900g/2lb	4 tbsp	100% (High)	20–22

Buckwheat

PRE-ROASTED: Place in a large cooking dish with boiling water and salt. Cover loosely with a lid or vented cling film and cook for first time and power setting. Reduce power setting and cook for second time specified, stirring 2–3 times. Leave to stand, covered, for 3–5 minutes before serving. Fluff with a fork to separate and serve.

Quantity	Water	Salt	1st Time/Power	2nd Time/Power
175g/6oz	600ml/1 pint	1 tsp	3 minutes/ 100% (High)	12 minutes/ 50% (Medium)

Bulghur

BULGHUR GRAINS (CRACKED WHEAT): Place in a large cooking dish with boiling water and salt. Cover loosely with a lid or vented cling film and cook for first time and power setting. Reduce power setting and cook for second time specified, stirring twice. Leave to stand, covered, for 3–5 minutes before serving. Fluff the grains with a fork to separate and serve.

Quantity	Water	Salt	1st Time/Power	2nd Time/Power
225g/8oz	500ml/18fl oz	1 tsp	3 minutes/ 100% (High)	9–12 minutes/ 50% (Medium)

Butter

TO SOFTEN: Place chilled butter in a dish and cook for the time specified, watching constantly.

Quantity	Power	Seconds
100g/4oz	100% (High)	15–30
250g/9oz	100% (High)	30

TO MELT: Place in a dish and cook for the time specified.

Quantity	Power	Minutes
25g/1oz	100% (High)	½
50g/2oz	100% (High)	1
100g/4oz	100% (High)	1¼–1½
225g/8oz	100% (High)	2–2½

Butter or Lima Beans (Dried)

TO COOK SOAKED BEANS: Place soaked beans in a cooking dish. Cover with boiling water. Cover and cook for the first time and power specified. Reduce the power setting and cook for the second time specified, adding extra boiling water to cover if needed. Drain to use as required.

Quantity	1st Time/Power	2nd Time/Power
225g/8oz	10 minutes/ 100% (High)	20–25 minutes/ 50% (Medium)

C

CABBAGE
CAKES
CANNELLINI BEANS
CARAMEL
CARROTS
CASSEROLES
CAULIFLOWER
CELERY
CHEESE
CHEESECAKE
CHEESE SAUCE
CHERRIES
CHICK PEAS
CHICKEN
CHICKEN LIVERS
CHINESE CABBAGE
CHOCOLATE
CHRISTMAS PUDDING
COCOA
COCONUT
COD
COFFEE
CORN ON THE COB AND CORN KERNELS
COTTAGE CHEESE
COURGETTES
COUSCOUS
CRABMEAT
CRANBERRIES
CRANBERRY SAUCE
CREAM
CRÊPES

CROISSANTS
CROÛTONS
CURLY KALE
CUSTARD

Cabbage

FRESH: Core and shred and place in a large dish so that the cabbage fits loosely. Add water, cover and cook for the specified time, stirring once. Leave to stand for 2 minutes before serving. Season after cooking.

Quantity	Water	Power	Minutes
225g/8oz	4 tbsp	100% (High)	7–9
450g/1lb	8 tbsp	100% (High)	9–11

FROZEN: Place in a large dish with the water. Cover and cook for the specified time, stirring once. Leave to stand for 2 minutes before serving. Season after cooking.

Quantity	Water	Power	Minutes
225g/8oz	4 tbsp	100% (High)	6–8
450g/1lb	8 tbsp	100% (High)	8–10

Cakes

FROZEN SMALL LIGHT FRUIT CAKE: To thaw, place on a rack and cook, uncovered, for the time specified, rotating twice. Leave to stand for 10 minutes before serving.

Quantity	Power	Minutes
1×small light fruit cake	20% (Defrost)	5
1 slice	20% (Defrost)	½–¾

FROZEN BLACK FOREST GÂTEAU: To thaw, place on a serving plate and cook, uncovered, for the time specified, checking constantly. Leave to stand for 30 minutes before serving.

Quantity	Power	Minutes
1 × 15cm/6 inch gâteau	20% (Defrost)	4–6

FROZEN CREAM SPONGE: To thaw, place on a double thickness sheet of absorbent kitchen towel and cook for the time specified. Leave to stand for 10–15 minutes before serving.

Quantity	Power	Minutes
1×15cm/6 inch sponge	100% (High)	¾

FROZEN JAM SPONGE: To thaw, place on a double thickness piece of absorbent kitchen towel and cook for the time specified. Leave to stand for 5 minutes before serving.

Quantity	Power	Minutes
1×15–18cm/6–7 inch sponge	20% (Defrost)	3

SMALL SPONGE BUNS: To thaw, place on a rack and cook for the time specified, checking frequently. Leave to stand for 5 minutes before serving.

Quantity	Power	Minutes
2	20% (Defrost)	1–1½
4	20% (Defrost)	1½–2

FROZEN CHOCOLATE ÉCLAIRS: To thaw, place on a double thickness sheet of absorbent kitchen towel and cook for the time specified. Leave to stand for 5–10 minutes before serving.

Quantity	Power	Minutes
2	20% (Defrost)	¾–1

FROZEN DOUGHNUTS: To thaw, place on a double thickness sheet of absorbent kitchen towel and cook for the time specified. Leave to stand for 3–5 minutes before serving.

Quantity	Power	Minutes
2×cream filled	20% (Defrost)	1–1½
2×jam filled	20% (Defrost)	1½–2

See also Victoria Sandwich (page 150)

Cannellini Beans (Dried) ———————————————

TO COOK SOAKED BEANS: Place soaked beans in a cooking dish. Cover with boiling water. Cover and cook for the first time and power specified. Reduce the power setting and cook for the second time specified, adding extra boiling water to cover if needed. Drain to use as required.

Quantity	1st Time/Power	2nd Time/Power
225g/8oz	10 minutes/ 100% (High)	20–25 minutes/ 50% (Medium)

Caramel

TO COOK: Place sugar and water in a large heatproof bowl. Cook for time specified, stirring once after 1 minute and watching carefully after 3 minutes' cooking time. Pour into an oiled mould (for crème caramel, for example) or on to an oiled sheet for pieces. Leave until cold.

Quantity	Water	Power	Minutes
50g/2oz	2 tbsp	100% (High)	3½–4

Carrots

FRESH BABY WHOLE AND SLICED: Place in a cooking dish with the water. Cover and cook for the time specified, stirring once. Leave to stand, covered, for 3–5 minutes before serving.

Quantity	Water	Power	Minutes
450g/1lb whole	4 tbsp	100% (High)	12–14
450g/1lb sliced	4 tbsp	100% (High)	10–12

FROZEN BABY WHOLE AND SLICED: Place in a cooking dish with the water. Cover and cook for the time specified, stirring once. Leave to stand, covered, for 2–3 minutes before serving.

Quantity	Water	Power	Minutes
450g/1lb whole	2 tbsp	100% (High)	10–12
450g/1lb sliced	2 tbsp	100% (High)	8–10

Casseroles

FROZEN: To thaw and reheat, place in a dish, cover and cook for the time specified, breaking up and stirring twice as the casserole thaws. Leave to stand, covered, for 3–5 minutes before serving.

Quantity	Power	Minutes
2 servings	100% (High)	8–10
4 servings	100% (High)	14–16

Cauliflower

FRESH WHOLE: Trim but leave whole, and place floret-side down in a dish with the water. Cover and cook for the time specified, turning over once. Leave to stand for 3–5 minutes before serving.

Quantity	Water	Power	Minutes
1×675g/1½lb whole	8 tbsp	50% (Medium)	13–17

FRESH FLORETS: Place in a dish with the water. Cover and cook for the time specified, stirring once. Leave to stand for 3 minutes before serving.

Quantity	Water	Power	Minutes
225g/8oz	3 tbsp	100% (High)	7–8
450g/1lb	4 tbsp	100% (High)	10–12

FROZEN FLORETS: To thaw and cook, place in a dish with the water. Cover and cook for the time specified, stirring once. Leave to stand for 2–3 minutes before serving.

Quantity	Water	Power	Minutes
225g/8oz	3 tbsp	100% (High)	5–6
450g/1lb	4 tbsp	100% (High)	8–9

Celery

FRESH SLICED: Slice into 5mm/¼ inch pieces and place in a shallow cooking dish. Add water and butter. Cover and cook for the time specified, stirring once. Leave to stand, covered, for 3 minutes before serving.

Quantity	Water	Butter	Power	Minutes
1 head/9 large sticks	2 tbsp	25g/1oz	100% (High)	5–6

FRESH CELERY HEARTS: Halve each heart lengthways and place in a shallow cooking dish. Add water and a knob of butter if preferred. Cover and cook for the time specified, turning once. Leave to stand, covered, for 3 minutes before serving.

Quantity	Water	Power	Minutes
4 hearts	2 tbsp	100% (High)	4½–5

CANNED: Place in a cooking dish with the thickest parts to the outer edge of the dish. Cover and cook for the power and time specified, stirring once.

Quantity	Power	Minutes
524g/1lb 2oz can	100% (High)	3

Cheese

TO RIPEN SEMI-SOFT CHEESES: Place on serving dish and cook for time specified depending upon degree of ripeness, checking constantly and turning after half the time. Leave to stand for 5 minutes before serving.

Quantity	Power	Seconds
225g/8oz	30% (Low)	15–45

TO SOFTEN CHILLED HARD CHEESES: Place on a serving dish and cook for time specified, turning over after half the time. Leave to stand for 5 minutes before serving.

Quantity	Power	Seconds
225g/8oz	30% (Low)	30–45

Cheesecake

FROZEN: To thaw, remove from container and place on a serving plate. Cook for the time specified, rotating once and checking frequently. Leave to stand for 5–15 minutes before serving.

Quantity	Power	Minutes
Family sized fruit topped	20% (Defrost)	5–6
Family sized cream topped	20% (Defrost)	1½–2
Individual fruit topped	20% (Defrost)	1–1½
Individual cream topped	20% (Defrost)	1–1¼

Cheese Sauce

TO MAKE BASIC POURING OR COATING SAUCE: Follow the instructions for white sauce on page 152. Add 50g/2oz grated cheese and a pinch of mustard powder for the last 2 minutes cooking time.

FROZEN: To thaw and reheat, place in a cooking dish, cover and cook for the time specified, stirring twice. Whisk to serve.

Quantity	Power	Minutes
300ml/½ pint	100% (High)	4–5

Cherries

POACHED IN LIGHT SYRUP: Prick and stone if preferred. Place in a cooking dish with 300ml/½ pint hot sugar-syrup. Cover loosely and cook for the time specified, stirring once. Leave to stand, covered, for 5 minutes. Serve hot or cold.

Quantity	Power	Minutes
450g/1lb	100% (High)	2–3

STEWED: Stone, wash and place in a cooking dish with the sugar and a little grated lemon rind if preferred. Cover and cook for the time specified, stirring once. Leave to stand, covered, for 3–5 minutes before serving.

Quantity	Sugar	Power	Minutes
450g/1lb	100g/4oz	100% (High)	4–5

FROZEN: Place in a dish, cover and cook for the time specified, stirring once. Leave to stand, covered, for 5 minutes before using.

Quantity	Power	Minutes
225g/8oz	20% (Defrost)	4–5
450g/1lb	20% (Defrost)	6–8

Chick Peas

TO COOK SOAKED PEAS: Place the soaked peas in a cooking dish. Cover with boiling water. Cover and cook for the first time and power specified. Reduce the power setting and cook for the second time specified, adding extra boiling water to cover if needed. Drain to use as required.

Quantity	1st Time/Power	2nd Time/Power
225g/8oz	10 minutes/	20–25 minutes/
	100% (High)	50% (Medium)

Chicken

TO COOK COATED DRUMSTICKS: Place on a roasting rack and cook for the time specified, turning over once. Leave to stand for 2–5 minutes before serving.

Quantity	Power	Minutes
2 medium	100% (High)	3–5
4 medium	100% (High)	8–10
8 medium	100% (High)	17–20

TO COOK PLAIN DRUMSTICKS: Remove the skin if preferred and place in a large dish, arranged bony side up with fleshiest parts to outside of dish. Cook for the time specified, turning over once. Leave to stand for 2–5 minutes before serving.

Quantity	Power	Minutes
2 medium	100% (High)	3–5
4 medium	100% (High)	8–9
8 medium	100% (High)	16–19

TO COOK CHICKEN THIGHS: Prick with a fork and place in a dish or on a roasting rack in a dish with the boniest parts to the centre of the dish. Cover with buttered greaseproof paper and cook for the time specified, turning over once. Crisp under a preheated hot grill if preferred.

Quantity	Power	Minutes
8 (1.25kg/2¾lb weight)	100% (High)	17–20

TO COOK CHICKEN QUARTER PORTIONS: Prick with a fork and brush with a glaze or browning agent if preferred. Place on a roasting rack in a dish, bony side up. Cover with buttered greaseproof paper and cook for the time specified, turning over once. Crisp under a preheated hot grill as desired.

Quantity	Power	Minutes
1	100% (High)	5–7
2	100% (High)	10–12
3	100% (High)	14–17
4	100% (High)	18–24

TO ROAST WHOLE FRESH CHICKEN: Truss chicken into a neat shape and shield the wing tips and legs with a little foil if necessary. Season with salt, pepper and herbs to taste and brush with a browning agent if preferred. Calculate all cooking times for birds after stuffing. Do not prick the skin, place breast-side down on a roasting rack or in a shallow cooking dish, and cook for the time specified, turning breast-side up half-way through the time. Cover with foil and leave to stand for 10–15 minutes. Prick with a fork to release excess juices and fat after cooking.

Quantity	Power	Minutes
1kg/2lb	100% (High)	12–16
1.5kg/3lb	100% (High)	18–24
1.8kg/4lb	100% (High)	25–36

FROZEN CHICKEN PIECES: To thaw, remove freezer wrappings and place on a roasting rack or in a shallow dish. Arrange so that the meatiest parts of the chicken pieces are to the outer edge of the dish. Cook for the time specified, turning over and rearranging once. Leave to stand for 10 minutes before using.

Quantity	Power	Minutes
2×225g/8oz quarters	30% (Low)	7–9
4×225g/8oz quarters	30% (Low)	15
2×100g/4oz drumsticks	30% (Low)	4–5
4×100g/4oz drumsticks	30% (Low)	7–8
6×100g/4oz drumsticks	30% (Low)	12
4×100g/4oz thighs	30% (Low)	8
8×100g/4oz thighs	30% (Low)	15
450g/1lb wings	30% (Low)	8
900g/2lb wings	30% (Low)	15
2×225g/8oz boneless breasts	30% (Low)	8
4×225g/8oz boneless breasts	30% (Low)	15

FROZEN WHOLE CHICKEN: To thaw, remove wrappings and place breast-side down on a roasting rack or shallow dish. Cook for the time specified, turning over halfway through the time and shielding legs, wing tips or hot spots with foil if necessary. Leave to stand for 15 minutes before using. Remove any giblets at the end of the defrosting time.

Quantity	Power	Minutes
1kg/2lb	20% (Defrost)	12–14
1.5kg/3lb	20% (Defrost)	18–22
1.8kg/4lb	20% (Defrost)	24–30

See also Poussins (page 118)

Chicken Livers

TO COOK FRESH OR DEFROSTED FROZEN: Prick thoroughly and place in a bowl with a little butter. Cover loosely and cook for the time specified, stirring twice.

Quantity	Power	Minutes
225g/8oz	100% (High)	2–3
450g/1lb	100% (High)	5–6

FROZEN: Remove from carton and place in a dish. Cover and cook for time specified, separating livers as they soften. Leave to stand, covered, for 5 minutes before using.

Quantity	Power	Minutes
1×225g/8oz carton	20% (Defrost)	6–8

Chinese Cabbage

FRESH: Slice and place in a large dish so that the cabbage fits loosely. Add water, cover and cook for the time specified, stirring once. Leave to stand for 3–5 minutes before serving. Season after cooking.

Quantity	Water	Power	Minutes
450g/1lb	2–3 tbsp	100% (High)	6–8

Chocolate

TO MELT: Break the chocolate into pieces and place in a bowl. Cook for time specified, stirring twice until smooth.

Quantity		Power	Minutes
Plain Dessert:	50g/2oz	50% (Medium)	2–2½
	100g/4oz	50% (Medium)	2½–3
	225g/8oz	50% (Medium)	3–3½
Milk Dessert:	50g/2oz	50% (Medium)	1¾–2¾
	100g/4oz	50% (Medium)	2½–3¼
	225g/8oz	50% (Medium)	3¼–4
Baking or Cooking:	50g/2oz	50% (Medium)	3–3½
	100g/4oz	50% (Medium)	4–4¼
	225g/8oz	50% (Medium)	5¼–5¾

Chocolate Chips:	50g/2oz	50% (Medium)	2½–3½
	100g/4oz	50% (Medium)	3½–4¼
	225g/8oz	50% (Medium)	4½–5¼
White:	50g/2oz	50% (Medium)	1¼–1¾
	100g/4oz	50% (Medium)	1½–2½
	225g/8oz	50% (Medium)	2½–3¼

Christmas Pudding

TO COOK: Place basic mixture into a greased pudding basin. Cover with vented cling film and cook for the time specified, rotating the basin twice. Leave to stand, covered, for 15 minutes before serving.

Quantity		Power	Minutes
Basic mixture to fit a			
1.2 litre/2 pint basin		100% (High)	8
(to serve 4–6)	or	30% (Low)	16–24

TO REHEAT: Cover loosely with cling film and cook for the time specified. Leave to stand, covered, for 3–4 minutes before serving.

Quantity	Power	Minutes
As above	100% (High)	2–3

Cocoa

Mix the sugar with the cocoa in a large jug. Add 150ml/¼ pint of the milk and cook for the first time specified. Add the remaining milk and cook for the second time specified. Serve at once.

Quantity	Sugar	Cocoa	Milk	Power	1st Time	2nd Time
2 cups	25g/1oz	4 tsp	450ml/ ¾ pint	100% (High)	1–1½ mins	1–2 mins
4 cups	50g/2oz	8 tsp	900ml/ 1½ pints	100% (High)	1–1½ mins	3 mins

Coconut

TO TOAST: Spread the desiccated coconut on a plate. Cook for the time specified, stirring once every minute until golden. Allow to cool before using.

Quantity	Power	Minutes
100g/4oz	100% (High)	5–6

Cod

STEAMED COD STEAKS: Fold or tuck in the end flaps of the cod steaks and secure into a neat shape with wooden cocktail sticks. Arrange in a large dish with sticks to the centre. Dot with a little butter and sprinkle with a little lemon juice. Cover with vented cling film and cook for time specified, rotating dish twice. Leave to stand, covered, for 2–3 minutes before serving.

Quantity	Power	Minutes
2×225g/8oz	100% (High)	5
4×225g/8oz	100% (High)	8–9

STEAMED COD FILLETS: Arrange the fish fillets in a large dish with the thicker portions to the outside of the dish. Dot with a little butter, sprinkle with lemon juice and season with pepper. Cover with vented cling film and cook for the time specified, rearranging once. Leave to stand, covered, for 3 minutes before serving.

Quantity	Power	Minutes
450g/1lb	100% (High)	5–7

POACHED COD FILLETS: Arrange the cod fillets in a large dish with the thicker portions to the outside of the dish. Season with pepper and lemon juice and pour over milk, water or stock. Cover with vented cling film and cook for the time specified, rearranging once. Leave to stand, covered, for 3 minutes before serving.

Quantity	Liquid	Power	Minutes
450g/1lb	8 tbsp	100% (High)	5–7

FROZEN COD STEAKS: To thaw, place in a dish, cover and cook for the time specified, turning over or rearranging once. Leave to stand for 10 minutes before using.

Quantity	Power	Minutes
1×225g/8oz	20% (Defrost)	2–2½
2×225g/8oz	20% (Defrost)	3–4
4×225g/8oz	20% (Defrost)	6–7

FROZEN COD FILLETS: To thaw, place in a dish with thicker portions to outer edge. Cover and cook for the time specified, rearranging once. Leave to stand for 5 minutes before using.

Quantity	Power	Minutes
450g/1lb	20% (Defrost)	7–8

Coffee

TO REHEAT READY-MADE FRESH BLACK COFFEE: Place cold coffee in a jug and cook for the time specified.

Quantity	Power	Minutes
600ml/1 pint	100% (High)	4½–5
1.2 litres/2 pints	100% (High)	7–7½

TO HEAT READY-MADE FRESH COLD BLACK COFFEE AND COLD MILK TOGETHER: Place in separate jugs and cook for the time specified.

Quantity	Power	Minutes
Coffee/Milk		
600ml/1 pint+		
150ml/¼ pint	100% (High)	5–5½
1.2 litres/2 pints+		
300ml/½ pint	100% (High)	8–8½

Corn on the Cob and Corn Kernels

FRESH UNHUSKED: Arrange on the base of the cooker or on turntable, evenly spaced. Cook for the time specified, rotating and rearranging once. Leave to stand for 5 minutes before removing husk, silky threads and woody base with a sharp knife.

Quantity	Power	Minutes
1×175–225g/6–8oz	100% (High)	3–5
2×175–225g/6–8oz	100% (High)	6–8
3×175–225g/6–8oz	100% (High)	8–10
4×175–225g/6–8oz	100% (High)	10–12

FRESH HUSKED: Wrap individually in cling film or place in a dish with 4 tablespoons water and cover. Place or arrange evenly in the microwave and cook for the time specified, rotating and rearranging once. Leave to stand, covered, for 3–5 minutes before serving.

Quantity	Power	Minutes
1×175–225g/6–8oz	100% (High)	3–4
2×175–225g/6–8oz	100% (High)	5–6
3×175–225g/6–8oz	100% (High)	7–8
4×175–225g/6–8oz	100% (High)	9–10

FROZEN CORN KERNELS: Place in a cooking dish with 4 tablespoons water. Cover and cook for the time specified, stirring once. Leave to stand, covered, for 2–3 minutes before serving.

Quantity	Power	Minutes
1×283g/10oz packet	100% (High)	5–6
1×454g/1lb packet	100% (High)	7–8

CANNED CORN KERNELS: Drain off all but 2 tablespoons can juice. Place in a cooking dish with the liquid. Cover and cook for time specified, stirring once.

Quantity	Power	Minutes
1×298g/10½oz can	100% (High)	2–3
1×340g/12oz can	100% (High)	2½–3

CREAMED CORN KERNELS: Place in a cooking dish. Cover and cook for time specified, stirring once.

Quantity	Power	Minutes
1×298g/10½oz can	100% (High)	2–3
1×340g/12oz can	100% (High)	2½–3

Cottage Cheese

TO MAKE FRESH: Place the milk in a bowl and cook, uncovered, for the first time and power specified. Stir in the rennet and cook for the second time specified or until the milk has set. Stir to separate the curds from the whey. Place in a muslin-lined sieve, tie to enclose and suspend to drain overnight. Season or flavour the cottage cheese as liked. Makes about 100g/3½oz.

Milk	Rennet	1st Time/Power	2nd Time/Power
600ml/1 pint	1½ tbsp	1½–2 minutes/ 100% (High)	4–5 minutes/ 30% (Low)

Courgettes

FRESH: Top and tail and slice thinly. Place in a shallow cooking dish with butter. Cover loosely and cook for the time specified, stirring once. Leave to stand, covered, for 2–3 minutes before serving.

Quantity	Butter	Power	Minutes
225g/8oz	25g/1oz	100% (High)	4–6½
450g/1lb	40g/1½oz	100% (High)	6–8

FROZEN: Place in a shallow cooking dish with butter if preferred. Cover loosely and cook for the time specified, stirring once. Leave to stand, covered, for 2–3 minutes before serving.

Quantity	Butter	Power	Minutes
450g/1lb	40g/1½oz	100% (High)	7–8

Couscous

PRE-COOKED: Place in a cooking dish with warm water. Leave to soak for 10 minutes. Add butter and salt to taste. Cook for time specified, stirring every 3–4 minutes. Leave to stand, covered, for 2–3 minutes before serving.

Quantity	Water	Butter	Power	Minutes
350g/12oz (to serve 4)	250ml/8fl oz	50g/2oz	50% (Medium)	15

Crabmeat

FROZEN TO THAW: Leave in wrappings. Cook for the time and power specified, turning over once. Leave to stand for 2 minutes then flake to use.

Quantity	Power	Minutes
225g/8oz	20% (Defrost)	4

Cranberries ———————————————

FROZEN: To thaw, place in a shallow dish and cook for the time specified, stirring once every minute. Use as required.

Quantity	Power	Minutes
175g/6oz	20% (Defrost)	3–4

Cranberry Sauce ———————————————

Place the cranberries, water and sugar in a large bowl. Cover with vented cling film and cook for time specified, stirring every 6 minutes, until pulpy. Serve warm or cold.

Quantity	Water	Sugar	Power	Minutes
450g/1lb	6 tbsp	350g/12oz	100% (High)	18–20

Cream ———————————————

FROZEN PIECES: To thaw, pierce the bag and place in a large bowl. Cook for the first time specified, turning the bag over once. Pour the cream from the bag into the bowl and cook for the second time specified, stirring once. Leave to stand, covered, for 5–10 minutes before using.

Quantity	Power	1st Time	2nd Time
1×575ml/1 pint bag	20% (Defrost)	5 minutes	3 minutes

DAIRY WHIPPED CREAM IN TUB: Remove lid if foil and re-cover with vented cling film. Cook for the time specified. Stir well and leave, covered, for 5 minutes before using.

Quantity	Power	Minutes
1×250ml/9fl oz tub	20% (Defrost)	2½–3

Crêpes ———————————————

Since it is impossible to make crêpes in a microwave, the instructions here are for reheating crêpes made in the usual way in a frying pan.

CONVENTIONALLY-MADE: To reheat until hot, stack 8 crêpes on a plate. Cover with cling film and cook for the specified time. Use as required.

Quantity	Power	Minutes
8	100% (High)	¾–1

CONVENTIONALLY-MADE FROZEN: To thaw, place a stack of 8 crêpes on a plate and cook for the time specified, rotating once. Leave to stand for 5 minutes then peel apart.

Quantity	Power	Minutes
8	50% (Medium)	1½–2

Croissants

TO WARM: Place on a double thickness piece of absorbent kitchen towel and cook for the time specified.

Quantity	Power	Minutes
4	100% (High)	¼–½

FROZEN: To thaw, place on a double thickness piece of absorbent kitchen paper and cook for the time specified.

Quantity	Power	Minutes
2	20% (Defrost)	½–1
4	20% (Defrost)	1½–2

Croûtons

DRY – OIL FREE: Remove crusts and dice bread into 1.5cm/½ inch cubes. Place on a large flat plate. Cook for the time specified until dry, stirring once every minute.

Quantity	Power	Minutes
175g/6oz	100% (High)	3–4

BUTTER CRISP: Place butter in a dish and cook for first time specified. Add bread cubes and toss to coat. Cook for the second time specified until crisp and brown, stirring once every minute.

Quantity	Butter	Power	1st Time	2nd Time
175g/6oz	25g/1oz	100% (High)	½ minute	3–4 minutes

Curly Kale

FRESH: Remove the thick stalk and stems, and shred. Place in a large dish with the water. Cover and cook for the specified time, stirring every 5 minutes. Leave to stand for 2 minutes before serving.

Quantity	Water	Power	Minutes
450g/1lb	150ml/¼ pint	100% (High)	15–17

Custard

POURING: Place milk in a jug and cook for the first time and power specified. Beat the egg yolks and sugar in a bowl and gradually add the hot milk. Cook for the second time and power specified, stirring once every minute until thick enough to coat the back of a spoon. Flavour with vanilla essence if preferred.

Milk	1st Time and Power	Egg Yolks	Sugar	2nd Time and Power
600ml/1 pint	4 minutes 100% (High)	4	3 tbsp	5–6 minutes 70% (Medium/High)

BAKED: Place milk in a bowl and cook for the first time and power specified. Beat the eggs and sugar and mix with the milk. Strain into 4 individual dishes and cook for the second time and power specified, turning 3 times and rearranging once. Leave to stand for 10 minutes.

Milk	1st Time and Power	Eggs	Sugar	2nd Time and Power
450ml/¾ pint	1 minute 100% (High)	3	3 tbsp	10–14 minutes 50% (Medium)

D

DAMSONS
DELICATESSEN BOILING SAUSAGES
DRIED BEANS
DRIED FRUIT SALAD
DUCK

Damsons

POACHED IN LIGHT SYRUP: Prick whole damsons or halve and stone them. Place in a cooking dish with 300ml/½ pint hot sugar syrup. Cover loosely and cook for the time specified, stirring once. Leave to stand, covered, for 5 minutes. Serve hot or cold.

Quantity	Power	Minutes
450g/1lb whole	100% (High)	3
450g/1lb halved	100% (High)	2

STEWED: Stone and wash. Place in a cooking dish with the sugar and a little grated lemon rind if desired. Cover and cook for the time specified, stirring once. Leave to stand, covered, for 3–5 minutes before serving.

Quantity	Sugar	Power	Minutes
450g/1lb	100g/4oz	100% (High)	4–5

FROZEN WHOLE: Place in a cooking dish. Cover and cook for the time specified, stirring once. Leave to stand, covered, for 5–10 minutes before using.

Quantity	Power	Minutes
225g/8oz	20% (Defrost)	4–5
450g/1lb	20% (Defrost)	7–8

Delicatessen Boiling Sausages

TO COOK: Puncture the boiling sausage while still in its bag. Place on a dish and cook for time specified, turning over once. Leave to stand for 5 minutes before removing from bag to serve.

Quantity	Power	Minutes
1×241g/8½oz	100% (High)	2–3
2×241g/8½oz	100% (High)	4

Dried Beans

TO HASTEN SOAKING PRIOR TO COOKING: Place in a cooking dish, cover with boiling water. Cover and cook for 5 minutes at 100% (High). Leave to stand for 1½ hours before draining and rinsing to cook.

Dried Fruit Salad

Place in a dish with fruit juice and water. Cover and cook for first time specified, stirring twice. Leave to stand and cool for 1 hour. Stir in sugar and cook for second time specified. Serve warm or chilled.

Quantity	Fruit Juice	Water	Sugar	Power	1st Time	2nd Time
450g/1lb	600ml/ 1 pint	600ml/ 1 pint	75g/ 3oz	100% (High)	10 minutes	6 minutes

Duck

TO ROAST WHOLE: Remove any fat from inside the body. Secure any tail-end flaps of skin to the main body with wooden cocktail sticks. Shield the wing tips and legs with foil as necessary, for half the cooking time. Prick the skin thoroughly and baste with browning agent or glaze if preferred. Place breast-side down on a roasting rack in a dish and cook for the first time specified. Turn over, breast-side up, and drain away any excess fat. Glaze again if preferred and cook for the second time specified. Drain again to remove excess fat and cook for the third time specified. Leave to stand, covered with foil, for 5 minutes before serving. Crisp the skin under a preheated hot grill as desired.

Quantity	Power	1st Time	2nd Time	3rd Time
1×2.25kg/5lb or 7–8 minutes per 450g/1lb	100% (High)	10 minutes	15 minutes	10–15 minutes

TO ROAST PORTIONS: Make deep diagonal cuts into the skin of the duck and place, skin-side up, on a roasting rack over a dish. Glaze or baste with a browning agent if preferred. Cover and cook for the time specified, turning over and rearranging once. Leave to stand, covered, for 10 minutes before serving. Crisp under a preheated hot grill as desired.

Quantity	Power	Minutes
4×350–400g/12–14oz portions	100% (High)	20–25

TO ROAST DUCK FILLETS: Make deep diagonal cuts into the skin of the duck fillets and place, skin-side up, on a roasting rack over a dish. Glaze or baste with a browning agent if preferred. Cover and cook for the time specified, turning and rearranging once. Leave to stand, covered, for 5 minutes before serving. Crisp under a preheated hot grill as desired.

Quantity	Power	Minutes
4×175g/6oz fillets	70% (Medium/High)	15–20

TO COOK DUCK FILLETS IN A BROWNING DISH: Make deep diagonal cuts into the skin of the duck fillets. Preheat a browning dish according to the manufacturer's instructions: about 5 minutes. Place the duck, skin-side down, on the dish and cook, uncovered, for first time specified. Turn over and cook for second time specified, turning over once. Leave to stand, covered, for 5 minutes before serving. Crisp under a preheated hot grill as desired.

Quantity	Power	1st Time	2nd Time
4×175g/6oz fillets	100% (High)	3 minutes	10 minutes

FROZEN WHOLE: To defrost, shield the wing tips, tail end and legs with foil as necessary, for half the cooking time. Place, breast-side down, in a shallow dish and cook for the first time specified. Turn breast-side up and cook for the second time specified, rotating twice. Leave to stand, covered, for 15 minutes before using. Remove giblets from duck cavity as soon as they loosen sufficiently.

Quantity	Power	1st Time	2nd Time
1×2.25kg/5lb or 5–6 minutes per 450g/1lb	20% (Defrost)	10 minutes	15–20 minutes

FROZEN DUCK PORTIONS: To defrost, place in a dish and cook for first time and power specified. Turn over, rearrange and cook for second time and power specified. Leave to stand, covered, for 15 minutes before using.

Quantity	1st Time/Power	2nd Time/Power
4×350–400g/12–14oz portions	7 minutes/ 100% (High)	10–14 minutes/ 20% (Defrost)

E

EGGS

Eggs

FRIED: Preheat a browning dish according to the manufacturer's instructions: about 1 minute per egg. Add a knob of butter and swirl to coat the base of the dish. Break the eggs into the dish, pierce the yolks quickly, cover and cook for the specified time. Leave to stand for 1–2 minutes then serve.

Quantity	Power	Minutes
1	100% (High)	½–¾
2	100% (High)	1½–1¾
4	100% (High)	2–2¼
or		
1	50% (Medium)	¾–1
2	50% (Medium)	1½–2
4	50% (Medium)	2–2½

POACHED: Place 2 tablespoons water and ¼ teaspoon vinegar into each ramekin dish used (one egg per ramekin). Cook at 100% (High) until the water is boiling, about ½ minute for 1 ramekin, ¾ minute for 2, 1¼–1½ minutes for 4–6. Break each egg into a ramekin and quickly prick or pierce the yolks. Cover and cook for the specified time, turning every ¾ minute. Leave to stand, covered, for 2–3 minutes before serving.

Quantity	Power	Minutes
1	50% (Medium)	¾–1
2	50% (Medium)	1¼–1½
3	50% (Medium)	2½–3
4	50% (Medium)	3½–4

SCRAMBLED: Place the butter in a jug or bowl and cook at 100% (High) until melted: about ½–1 minute. Add the eggs and milk and cook for half the specified time. Stir the set pieces of egg from the outside of the bowl to the centre, then cook for the remaining specified time, stirring twice. Leave to stand for 1–2 minutes before serving.

Quantity	Butter	Milk	Power	Minutes
1	1 tsp	1 tbsp	100% (High)	¾–1
2	15g/½oz	2 tbsp	100% (High)	2–2¼
4	15g/½oz	2 tbsp	100% (High)	2½–3
6	25g/1oz	4 tbsp	100% (High)	3¼–4
8	25g/1oz	4 tbsp	100% (High)	4½–5

BAKED: Crack each egg into either a buttered microwave bun tray or buttered small glass cup or ramekin dish. Pierce the yolks quickly, cover with vented cling film and cook for half the specified time. Give the dishes a half turn then cook for the remaining specified time.

Quantity	Power	Minutes
1	50% (Medium)	1–1¼
2	50% (Medium)	2–2¼
4	50% (Medium)	3½–4
6	50% (Medium)	5½–6

F

FENNEL
FISH CAKES
FISH FINGERS
FISH IN SAUCE
FISH ROES
FLAGEOLET BEANS
FLANS AND QUICHES
FRANKFURTERS
FRUIT CRUMBLE

Fennel

FRESH SLICED: Place in a cooking dish with the water. Cover and cook for the time specified, stirring once. Leave to stand, covered, for 2–3 minutes before serving.

Quantity	Water	Power	Minutes
450g/1lb	3 tbsp	100% (High)	9–10

Fish Cakes

TO COOK: Brush with melted butter if preferred. Place in a shallow dish, cover and cook for the time specified, turning over once. Leave to stand for 1–2 minutes before serving.

Quantity	Power	Minutes
4×75g/3oz	100% (High)	5

TO COOK IN BROWNING DISH: Preheat a browning dish according to the manufacturer's instructions: about 5 minutes at 100% (High). Add the fish cakes and cook for the time specified, turning over once.

Quantity	Power	Minutes
4×75g/3oz	100% (High)	5

FROZEN FISH CAKES: To thaw, unwrap and place in a shallow dish. Cover and cook for the time specified, rearranging once.

Quantity	Power	Minutes
4×75g/3oz	20% (Defrost)	5–6½

Fish Fingers

FROZEN: Preheat a microwave griddle or browning dish according to the manufacturer's instructions: about 6 minutes. Add the fish fingers and press down well. Cook for the time specified, turning over halfway through the cooking time. Leave to stand for 1–2 minutes before serving.

Quantity	Power	Minutes
2	100% (High)	1½
4	100% (High)	2
6	100% (High)	3
8	100% (High)	4

Fish in Sauce

TO COOK FROZEN BOIL-IN-THE-BAG FISH-IN-SAUCE: Pierce the bag and place on a plate. Cook for the time specified. Shake gently to mix, leave to stand for 2 minutes then snip open to serve.

Quantity	Power	Minutes
1 × 170g/6oz	20% (Defrost)	11–12
2 × 170g/6oz	50% (Medium)	10–12

Fish Roes

TO COOK FRESH: Place rinsed, soft fish roes (herring, for example) into a small dish with melted butter and salt and pepper to taste. Cover and cook for the time specified, stirring once. Leave to stand, covered, for 2 minutes before serving.

Quantity	Butter	Power	Minutes
100g/4oz	1 tbsp	30% (Low)	4–4½
225g/8oz	2 tbsp	30% (Low)	6–8

Flageolet Beans (Dried)

TO COOK SOAKED BEANS: Place soaked beans in a cooking dish. Cover with boiling water. Cover and cook for the first time and power specified. Reduce the power setting and cook for the second time specified, adding extra boiling water to cover if needed. Drain to use as required.

Quantity	1st Time/Power	2nd Time/Power
225g/8oz	10 minutes/ 100% (High)	20–25 minutes/ 50% (Medium)

Flans and Quiches

TO COOK FLAN CASE: Roll out 175g/6oz shortcrust pastry to a round large enough to line a 20cm/8 inch dish. Press in firmly, taking care not to stretch. Cut the pastry away, leaving a 5mm/¼ inch 'collar' above the dish to allow for any shrinkage. Prick the base and sides well with a fork. Place a double thickness layer of absorbent kitchen towel over the base, easing it into position round the edges. Cook for the first time specified, giving the dish a quarter turn once every minute. Remove the paper and cook for the second time specified. Fill as required.

Quantity	Power	1st Time	2nd Time
1×20cm/8 inch	100% (High)	3½ minutes	1½ minutes

ADDING UNCOOKED FILLING: If the flan case is then filled with a beaten egg mixture, with savoury or sweet ingredients, it is usually cooked for the time specified below, turning the dish every 3 minutes (although refer to specific recipe instructions). Leave to stand for 10–15 minutes to finish cooking.

Quantity	Power	Minutes
1×20cm/8 inch flan with 3 egg filling	20% (Defrost)	14–16

FROZEN UNFILLED COOKED FLANS: To thaw, place on a plate and cook for the time specified. Leave to stand for 5 minutes before using.

Quantity	Power	Minutes
1×15–18cm/6–7 inch	20% (Defrost)	1–1½

FROZEN FILLED COOKED FLANS: To thaw, place on a plate and cook for the time specified. Leave to stand for 5 minutes before using.

Quantity	Power	Minutes
1×10cm/4 inch	100% (High)	1½–2
1×20cm/8 inch	100% (High)	2½–3½

TO REHEAT COOKED FLANS: Place on a plate and cook for the time specified. Leave to stand for 3 minutes before serving.

Quantity	Power	Minutes
1×10cm/4 inch	100% (High)	1–1½
1×20cm/8 inch	100% (High)	2

Frankfurters ─────────────────────────────

CANNED IN BRINE: Drain and place on a roasting rack. Prick or slash diagonally and cook for the time specified, turning over once.

Quantity	Power	Minutes
1×425g/15oz can	100% (High)	2–3

VACUUM PACKED OR LOOSE: Prick or slash diagonally and place in a dish or on a roasting rack. Cook for the time specified, turning over once.

Quantity	Power	Minutes
2	100% (High)	1–2
4	100% (High)	3–4
6	100% (High)	4–5
450g/1lb	100% (High)	7–9

Fruit Crumble ─────────────────────────────

TO COOK: Place 900g/2lb prepared fruit (sliced apples, blackberries or sliced rhubarb, for example) in a dish, with sugar to taste. Sprinkle a 175g/6oz crumble mixture on top (made with 175g/6oz flour, 75g/3oz butter and 60g/2½oz sugar). Cook for time specified, turning dish 3 times. Leave to stand for 5 minutes before serving. Brown under a preheated hot grill if preferred.

Quantity	Power	Minutes
As above (to serve 4)	100% (High)	14–16

FROZEN: Cook frozen cooked or uncooked crumbles for first time and power specified, then for second time and power specified until cooked or reheated.

Quantity	1st Time/Power	2nd Time/Power
As above *cooked*	15 minutes/ 20% (Defrost)	5 minutes/ 100% (High)
As above *uncooked*	15 minutes/ 20% (Defrost)	10–14 minutes/ 100% (High)

G

GAME BIRDS
GAMMON
GARLIC BREAD
GIBLETS
GOOSEBERRIES
GRAPEFRUIT
GRAPES
GRAVY
GREEN PEAS
GREENGAGES

Game Birds _____

FRESH WHOLE ROAST GROUSE, GUINEA FOWL, PARTRIDGE, PHEASANT, PIGEON, QUAIL AND WOODCOCK: Rinse and dry then brush with a browning agent if preferred. Place on a roasting rack, breast-side down, cover loosely with greaseproof paper and cook for half the time specified. Rearrange and turn breast-side up, re-cover and cook for the remaining time. Allow to stand, covered, for 5 minutes before serving.

Quantity	Power	Minutes
1×450g/1lb	100% (High)	9–10
2×450g/1lb	100% (High)	20–22
1×900g/2lb	100% (High)	20–22
4×450g/1lb	100% (High)	35–40

FROZEN WHOLE GAME BIRDS: To thaw, place on a plate or in a shallow dish, breast-side down. Cover loosely and cook for half the recommended time. Turn breast-side up, rearrange if more than 1 bird, and cook for the remaining time. Allow to stand, covered, for 5–10 minutes before using.

Quantity	Power	Minutes
1×450g/1lb	20% (Defrost)	6–7
2×450g/1lb	20% (Defrost)	12–14
1×900g/2lb	20% (Defrost)	12–14
4×450g/1lb	20% (Defrost)	24–28

Gammon _____

BRAISED GAMMON STEAKS: Remove the rind and scissor-snip the fat of the gammon steaks. Place in a large shallow dish. Add the wine, cider or fruit juice and marinate for 1 hour if desired. Cover and cook for time specified, rearranging once. Leave to stand, covered, for 5 minutes before serving.

Quantity	Wine/Cider/Juice	Power	Minutes
4×100g/4oz steaks	150ml/¼ pint	100% (High)	4

READY-COOKED GAMMON JOINT: Remove any skin from the ready-cooked gammon joint and score the fat into a diamond pattern. Sprinkle with a little brown sugar and stud with cloves if preferred. Place in a shallow dish and cook, uncovered, for time specified, turning and rotating once. Leave to stand, covered loosely with foil, for 5–10 minutes before serving.

Quantity	Power	Minutes
1.5–1.8kg/3–4lb ready-cooked gammon joint	100% (High)	10

TO COOK RAW GAMMON JOINT: Place in a pierced roasting bag into a dish. Cover and cook for 12–14 minutes per 450g/1lb at 100% (High) turning over half-way through the cooking time. Cover with foil and leave to stand for 10 minutes before carving.

Quantity	Power	Minutes
450g/1lb joint	100% (High)	12–14
900g/2lb joint	100% (High)	24–28
1.5kg/3lb joint	100% (High)	36–42
1.75kg/4lb joint	100% (High)	48–56

FROZEN UNCOOKED GAMMON JOINT: To thaw, place the joint on a plate and cook for the time specified, turning over once. Leave to stand, covered, for 10–15 minutes before using.

Quantity	Power	Minutes
450g/1lb	20% (Defrost)	4–5
900g/2lb	20% (Defrost)	8–10

FROZEN GAMMON STEAKS: To thaw, place on a plate and cook for the time specified, turning over once. Leave to stand for 5 minutes before using.

Quantity	Power	Minutes
2×100g/4oz	20% (Defrost)	3–5
4×100g/4oz	20% (Defrost)	7–9

Garlic Bread _____

Using a short, crusty French stick or Vienna loaf, make diagonal slits, almost to the base of the loaf but not quite through, about 4cm/1½ inches apart. Spread the garlic butter (or savoury butter with herbs, if preferred) between the slits and re-form the loaf into a neat shape. Loosely wrap in absorbent kitchen towel and cook for the time specified. Serve at once while warm.

Quantity	Power	Minutes
100g/4oz	100% (High)	1½

Giblets

TO MAKE STOCK FOR GRAVY: Place giblets in a bowl with boiling water and a few sliced seasoning vegetables (carrots, celery and onion, for example). Cook for the time specified. Strain to use.

Quantity	Water	Power	Minutes
1 bag from poultry bird	300ml/½ pint	100% (High)	7–10

FROZEN: To thaw, place in a bowl, cover, and cook for time specified. Use as required.

Quantity	Power	Minutes
1 bag from poultry bird	20% (Defrost)	2–3

Gooseberries

FRESH: Top and tail and place in a cooking dish with the water. Cover and cook for the time specified. Stir in the sugar and leave to stand, covered, for 5 minutes.

Quantity	Water	Sugar	Power	Minutes
450g/1lb	2 tbsp	100g/4oz	100% (High)	4–6

FROZEN: To thaw, place in a dish and cook for the time specified, stirring once. Leave to stand for 5 minutes.

Quantity	Power	Minutes
450g/1lb	20% (Defrost)	8–10

Grapefruit

TO SERVE HOT: Cut grapefruit in half and, using a knife, loosen the segments. Top with a little sugar and spice and a cherry if preferred. Place in a dish and cook, uncovered, for the time specified, rotating the dish twice. Serve at once.

Quantity	Power	Minutes
2 whole, halved	100% (High)	3

FROZEN SEGMENTS IN SYRUP: Place in a dish, cover and cook for the time specified, separating the fruit as it thaws. Leave to stand, covered, for 10 minutes before serving.

Quantity	Power	Minutes
225g/8oz	20% (Defrost)	7–8
450g/1lb	20% (Defrost)	9–12

Grapes

FROZEN SEEDLESS IN SYRUP: Place in a dish, cover and cook for the time specified, separating the fruit as it thaws. Leave to stand, covered, for 5–10 minutes before serving.

Quantity	Power	Minutes
225g/8oz	20% (Defrost)	4–5
450g/1lb	20% (Defrost)	8–10

Gravy

Place pan juices or meat drippings into a bowl and stir in flour (depending upon thickness required). Cook for first time specified according to light or dark golden colour required. Gradually add the stock, blending well. Cook for second time specified, stirring once every minute until smooth, boiling and thickened. Season to serve.

Quantity	Flour	Power	1st Time	2nd Time
2 tbsp	1–2 tbsp	100% (High)	1–3 minutes	2–3 minutes

Green Peas (Whole Dried)

TO COOK SOAKED PEAS: Place soaked peas in a cooking dish. Cover with boiling water, cover and cook for the first time and power specified. Reduce the power setting and cook for the second time specified, adding extra boiling water to cover if needed. Drain to use as required.

Quantity	1st Time/Power	2nd Time/Power
225g/8oz	10 minutes/ 100% (High)	10–15 minutes/ 50% (Medium)

Greengages

POACHED IN LIGHT SYRUP: Prick whole greengages, or halve and stone them. Place in a cooking dish with 300ml/½ pint hot sugar-syrup. Cover loosely and cook for the time specified, stirring once. Leave to stand, covered, for 5 minutes. Serve hot or cold.

Quantity	Power	Minutes
450g/1lb whole	100% (High)	3
450g/1lb halved	100% (High)	2

STEWED: Stone and wash. Place in a cooking dish with the sugar and a little grated lemon rind if preferred. Cover and cook for the time specified, stirring once. Leave to stand, covered, for 3–5 minutes before serving.

Quantity	Sugar	Power	Minutes
450g/1lb	100g/4oz	100% (High)	4–5

FROZEN WHOLE: Place in a cooking dish. Cover and cook for the time specified, stirring once. Leave to stand, covered, for 10 minutes before using.

Quantity	Power	Minutes
225g/8oz	20% (Defrost)	5–6
450g/1lb	20% (Defrost)	8–9

H

HADDOCK
HALIBUT
HAM
HAMBURGERS
HARICOT BEANS
HAZELNUTS
HERBS
HERRING
HOLLANDAISE SAUCE
HONEY
HOT DOG

Haddock

STEAMED HADDOCK STEAKS: Fold or tuck in the end flaps of the haddock steaks and secure into a neat shape with wooden cocktail sticks. Arrange, with sticks to the centre, in a large dish. Dot with a little butter and sprinkle with a little lemon juice. Cover with vented cling film and cook for time specified, rotating dish twice. Leave to stand, covered, for 2–3 minutes before serving.

Quantity	Power	Minutes
2×225g/8oz	100% (High)	5
4×225g/8oz	100% (High)	8–9

STEAMED HADDOCK FILLETS: Arrange the fish fillets in a large dish with the thicker portions to the outside. Dot with a little butter, sprinkle with lemon juice and season with pepper. Cover with vented cling film and cook for the time specified, rearranging once. Leave to stand, covered, for 3 minutes before serving.

Quantity	Power	Minutes
450g/1lb	100% (High)	5–7

POACHED HADDOCK FILLETS: Arrange the fillets in a large dish with the thicker portions to the outside. Season with pepper and lemon juice and pour over milk, water or stock. Cover with vented cling film and cook for the time specified, rearranging once. Leave to stand, covered, for 3 minutes before serving.

Quantity	Liquid	Power	Minutes
450g/1lb	8 tbsp	100% (High)	5–7

FROZEN HADDOCK STEAKS: To thaw, place in a dish, cover and cook for the time specified, turning over or rearranging once. Leave to stand for 10 minutes before using.

Quantity	Power	Minutes
1×225g/8oz	20% (Defrost)	2–2½
2×225g/8oz	20% (Defrost)	3–4
4×225g/8oz	20% (Defrost)	6–7

FROZEN HADDOCK FILLETS: To thaw, place in a dish with thicker portions to outer edge. Cover and cook for the time specified, re-arranging once. Leave to stand for 5 minutes before using.

Quantity	Power	Minutes
450g/1lb	20% (Defrost)	7–8

Halibut

STEAMED HALIBUT STEAKS: Fold or tuck in the end flaps of the halibut steaks and secure into a neat shape with wooden cocktail sticks. Arrange, with sticks to the centre, in a large dish. Dot with a little butter and sprinkle with a little lemon juice. Cover with vented cling film and cook for time specified, rotating dish twice. Leave to stand, covered, for 2–3 minutes before serving.

Quantity	Power	Minutes
2×225g/8oz	100% (High)	4–5
4×225g/8oz	100% (High)	7½–8

FROZEN HALIBUT STEAKS: To thaw, place in a dish, cover and cook for the time specified, turning over or rearranging once. Leave to stand for 10 minutes before using.

Quantity	Power	Minutes
1×225g/8oz	20% (Defrost)	2–2½
2×225g/8oz	20% (Defrost)	3–4
4×225g/8oz	20% (Defrost)	6–7

Ham

COOKING/REHEATING READY-COOKED HAM (to eat hot): Place joint in a shallow dish or on a roasting rack. Cover and cook for time specified, turning over once. Cover loosely with foil and leave to stand for 5–10 minutes before serving.

Quantity	Power	Minutes
450g/1lb joint	50% (Medium)	13–17
900g/2lb joint	50% (Medium)	26–34
1.5kg/3lb joint	50% (Medium)	39–51
1.75kg/4lb joint	50% (Medium)	52–68

Above 2.25kg/5lb not recommended.

REHEATING CANNED HAM (to eat hot): Place joint in a shallow dish or on a roasting rack. Cover and cook for the time specified, turning over once. Cover loosely with foil and leave to stand for 5–10 minutes before serving.

Quantity	Power	Minutes
450g/1lb joint	50% (Medium)	10–12
900g/2lb joint	50% (Medium)	20–24
1.5kg/3lb joint	50% (Medium)	30–36
1.75kg/4lb joint	50% (Medium)	40–48

Above 2.25kg/5lb not recommended.

COOKING RAW HAM JOINTS: Place in a pierced roasting bag in a dish. Cover and cook for 12–14 minutes per 450g/1lb at 100% (High) turning over halfway through the cooking time. Cover with foil and leave to stand for 10 minutes before carving.

Quantity	Power	Minutes
450g/1lb joint	100% (High)	12–14
900g/2lb joint	100% (High)	24–28
1.5kg/3lb joint	100% (High)	36–42
1.75kg/4lb joint	100% (High)	48–56

FROZEN UNCOOKED HAM JOINT: To thaw, place the joint on a plate and cook for the time specified, turning over once. Leave to stand, covered, for 10–15 minutes before using.

Quantity	Power	Minutes
450g/1lb	20% (Defrost)	4–5
900g/2lb	20% (Defrost)	8–10

FROZEN SLICED COOKED HAM: To thaw, place on a plate and cook for the time specified, turning over once. Leave to stand for 5 minutes before using.

Quantity	Power	Minutes
1×100g/4oz packet	20% (Defrost)	3–4

Hamburgers

TO COOK: Place the burgers on a roasting rack and brush with browning agent if desired. Cook, uncovered, for the time specified, turning over once. Leave to stand for 2–3 minutes before serving.

Quantity	Power	Minutes
1×100g/4oz	100% (High)	3–4
2×100g/4oz	100% (High)	4–5
3×100g/4oz	100% (High)	5–6
4×100g/4oz	100% (High)	6–7

TO COOK IN A BROWNING DISH: Preheat a browning dish according to the manufacturer's instructions: about 5 minutes at 100% (High). Add the burgers and cook for the time specified, turning over once. Leave to stand for 2–3 minutes before serving.

Quantity	Power	Minutes
1×100g/4oz	100% (High)	2½–3
2×100g/4oz	100% (High)	3½–4
3×100g/4oz	100% (High)	4½–5
4×100g/4oz	100% (High)	5–5½

FROZEN HAMBURGERS: To thaw, place on absorbent kitchen towel and cook for the time specified, turning over and rearranging twice. Leave to stand for 2–3 minutes before using.

Quantity	Power	Minutes
4×100g/4oz	20% (Defrost)	10–12

Haricot Beans

TO COOK SOAKED BEANS: Place soaked beans in a cooking dish. Cover with boiling water. Cover and cook for the first time and power specified. Reduce the power setting and cook for the second time specified, adding extra boiling water to cover if needed. Drain to use as required.

Quantity	1st Time/Power	2nd Time/Power
225g/8oz	10 minutes/ 100% (High)	20–25 minutes/ 50% (Medium)

Hazelnuts

TO TOAST AND SKIN: Place hazelnuts on a large flat dish. Cook for time specified, stirring twice. Rub in a cloth to remove the skins.

Quantity	Power	Minutes
25–50g/1–2oz	100% (High)	2–2½

Herbs

TO DRY: Trim and sort, wash and dry and measure loosely packed in a measuring jug. Spread on absorbent kitchen towel in a single layer. Place in the microwave with a small glass of water and cook for the time specified, stirring and rearranging every 2 minutes. Dry on fresh kitchen towel until cool then crumble to store in airtight jars. Store for 3–6 months in a cool, dry, dark place.

Quantity	Power	Minutes
300ml/½ pint	100% (High)	7–9

Herring

TO COOK FRESH: Remove heads and clean and gut. Slash the skin in 2 to 3 places to prevent bursting. Shield the tail end with a little foil if preferred. Place in a dish or on a roasting rack, season with salt, pepper and lemon juice if preferred, and cover with greaseproof paper. Cook for the calculated time according to weight, turning and rearranging once. Leave to stand, covered, for 2–3 minutes before serving.

Quantity	Power	Minutes
per 450g/1lb	100% (High)	3–4

FROZEN WHOLE HERRING: To thaw, place on a roasting rack or in a shallow dish and cook for the calculated time according to weight, turning over once. Leave to stand for 10 minutes before using.

Quantity	Power	Minutes
per 450g/1lb	20% (Defrost)	5–7

Hollandaise Sauce

Place the butter in a large jug and cook for first time and power specified. Whisk in the lemon juice, egg yolks, a pinch of mustard powder and salt and pepper to taste. Cook for second time and power specified, whisk and serve.

Butter	Lemon Juice	Egg Yolks	1st Time/Power	2nd Time/Power
100g/4oz	3 tbsp	2	1½ minutes/ 100% (High)	1 minute/ 50% (Medium)

Honey

TO SOFTEN OR MELT/REVITALIZE CRYSTALLIZED OR HARDENED: Place honey in a bowl or leave in jar and cook for the time specified, stirring once.

Quantity	Power	Time
2 tbsp	100% (High)	10 seconds
1×450g/1lb jar	100% (High)	1½–2 minutes

Hot Dog

Place a hot dog sausage in a long soft roll or bun and wrap in absorbent kitchen towel. Cook for the time specified, turning over once. Serve with mustard, ketchup or relish.

Quantity	Power	Minutes
1	100% (High)	½–¾

I

**ICE CREAM
IRISH COFFEE**

Ice Cream

TO SOFTEN FOR SERVING: Cook in the container for the time specified. Leave to stand, covered, for 1 minute before slicing or scooping to serve.

Quantity	Power	Minutes
1 litre/1¾ pints	50% (Medium)	½–1½

Irish Coffee

Place the sugar, whiskey (or other alcohol, as preferred) and cold black coffee into stemmed heatproof glasses. Cook for the time specified until very hot. Stir well and carefully pour the cream over the back of a spoon on to the coffee to float. Serve at once.

Quantity	Sugar	Whiskey	Coffee	Cream	Power	Minutes
1	2 tbsp	2 tbsp	150ml/¼ pint	1–2 tbsp	100% (High)	1½–2
2	4 tbsp	4 tbsp	300ml/½ pint	3–4 tbsp	100% (High)	2½–3
4	8 tbsp	8 tbsp	600ml/1 pint	7–8 tbsp	100% (High)	4–5

J

JELLY

Jelly

TABLETS: Break the jelly tablet into cubes and place in a bowl with the water. Cook for the time specified. Stir to dissolve, then make up with cold water according to packet instructions.

Quantity	Water	Power	Minutes
1×135g/4½oz packet	150ml/¼ pint	100% (High)	2
2×135g/4½oz packets	300ml/½ pint	100% (High)	3

K

**KIDNEYS
KIPPERS
KOHLRABI**

Kidneys

FRESH LAMB'S, PIG'S OR OX: Halve and core the kidneys. Preheat a browning dish according to the manufacturer's instructions: about 5 minutes at 100% (High). Add the oil and kidneys. Cook for the time specified, turning and rearranging after 2 minutes. Leave to stand, covered, for 3 minutes before serving.

Quantity	Oil	Power	Minutes
100g/4oz	1 tsp	100% (High)	4
225g/8oz	1 tsp	100% (High)	8
350g/12oz	1 tsp	100% (High)	12
450g/1lb	1 tsp	100% (High)	16

FROZEN LAMB'S, PIG'S OR OX: To thaw, place in a bowl, cover and cook for the time specified, stirring 3 times. Leave to stand, covered, for 5 minutes before using.

Quantity	Power	Minutes
2 lamb's	20% (Defrost)	1½–2
4 lamb's	20% (Defrost)	4
2 pig's	20% (Defrost)	4
4 pig's	20% (Defrost)	7–8
225g/8oz ox	20% (Defrost)	6
450g/1lb ox	20% (Defrost)	9–10

Kippers

FRESH: Remove heads and tails using scissors. Place, skin-side down, on a plate. Cover loosely and cook for the time specified, rearranging once.

Quantity	Power	Minutes
1	100% (High)	1–2
2	100% (High)	3–4
4	100% (High)	6–7

FROZEN KIPPER FILLETS: To thaw and cook, place the frozen cook-in-bag on a plate and snip a couple of vents in the bag. Cook for the time specified, turning over once.

Quantity	Power	Minutes
1×175g/6oz packet	100% (High)	5–6

Kohlrabi

TO COOK FRESH: Trim away the root ends and stems, scrub and peel the bulb and cut into 5mm/¼ inch slices. Place in a cooking dish with the water. Cover and microwave for the time and power specified, stirring twice. Leave to stand for 3–4 minutes then drain to serve.

Quantity	Water	Power	Minutes
450g/1lb slices	3 tbls	100% (High)	5–6
900g/2lb slices	5 tbls	100% (High)	9–11

L

LAMB
LASAGNE
LEEKS
LEMONS
LENTILS
LIVER
LOBSTER

Lamb

LAMB CHOPS COOKED IN BROWNING DISH: Preheat a large browning dish according to the manufacturer's instructions: about 5 minutes at 100% (High). Add the lamb chops so that the meatiest portions are to the outer edge of the dish. Cook for the time specified, turning over once. Leave to stand for 2 minutes before serving.

Quantity	Power	Minutes
2×100–175g/4–6oz loin	100% (High)	6–7
4×100–175g/4–6oz loin	100% (High)	8–9
2×100–175g/4–6oz chump	100% (High)	6–8
4×100–175g/4–6oz chump	100% (High)	8–10

TO COOK RACK OF LAMB: Place prepared rack of lamb (tied Guard of Honour style) on a roasting rack and season with salt, pepper and herbs if desired. Cook for the time specified, rotating the dish every 3 minutes. Cover with foil and leave to stand for 10 minutes before carving.

Quantity	Power	Minutes
1×1.2kg/2–2½lb rack with 7 ribs (to serve 3–4)	100% (High)	Rare: 12
		Medium: 13
		Well Done: 14½–15

TO ROAST JOINT: Place joint on a roasting rack and shield any thinly covered bone area with foil if necessary. Calculate the cooking time according to the joint type and size and cook for the first time and power specified, reduce power setting and cook for second time and power specified, turning over once. Cover with foil and leave to stand for 20 minutes before serving.

Quantity	Total Cooking Time (for calculation)	1st Time/Power	2nd Time/Power
Leg with bone	Rare: 8–10 minutes per 450g/1lb	5 minutes/ 100% (High)	remaining time/50% (Medium)
	Medium: 10–12 minutes per 450g/1lb	5 minutes/ 100% (High)	remaining time/50% (Medium)

	Well done: 12–14 minutes per 450g/1lb	5 minutes/ 100% (High)	remaining time/50% (Medium)
Boned joints	Rare: 10–12 minutes per 450g/1lb	5 minutes/ 100% (High)	remaining time/50% (Medium)
	Medium: 13–15 minutes per 450g/1lb	5 minutes/ 100% (High)	remaining time/50% (Medium)
	Well Done: 16–18 minutes per 450g/1lb	5 minutes/ 100% (High)	remaining time/50% (Medium)
Shoulder joints	Rare: 7–9 minutes per 450g/1lb	5 minutes/ 100% (High)	remaining time/50% (Medium)
	Medium: 9–11 minutes per 450g/1lb	5 minutes/ 100% (High)	remaining time/50% (Medium)
	Well Done: 11–13 minutes per 450g/1lb	5 minutes/ 100% (High)	remaining time/50% (Medium)

FROZEN LAMB CHOPS: To thaw, place on a roasting rack and cook for the time specified, turning and rearranging once. Leave to stand for 10 minutes before using.

Quantity	Power	Minutes
2×100–175g/4–6oz loin	20% (Defrost)	3–4
4×100–175g/4–6oz loin	20% (Defrost)	6–8
2×100–175g/4–6oz chump	20% (Defrost)	3–4
4×100–175g/4–6oz chump	20% (Defrost)	6–8

FROZEN UNCOOKED LAMB JOINT: To thaw, place the joint on a roasting rack in a dish and cook for the time calculated below, turning over once. Leave to stand, covered, for 30–45 minutes before using.

Quantity	Power	Minutes
Boned rolled joint	20% (Defrost)	5–6 minutes per 450g/1lb
Joints on bone	20% (Defrost)	5–6 minutes per 450g/1lb

Lasagne _____

TO THAW AND COOK FROZEN PREPARED: Remove from foil packaging if
necessary and place in a cooking dish. Cover and cook for the first
time and power specified. Allow to stand for 5 minutes then cook for
the second time and power specified. Brown under a preheated hot
grill if liked.

Quantity	1st Time/Power	2nd Time/Power
450g/1lb	8 minutes/	8–9 minutes/
	20% (Defrost)	100% (High)

Leeks _____

FRESH WHOLE: Trim and slit from the top of the white to the green
leaves in 2 to 3 places. Wash thoroughly and place in a cooking dish
with the water. Cover and cook for the time specified, rearranging
twice. Leave to stand, covered, for 3–5 minutes before serving.

Quantity	Water	Power	Minutes
450g/1lb	3 tbsp	100% (High)	3–5
900g/2lb	5 tbsp	100% (High)	6–8

FRESH SLICED: Place in a cooking dish with the water. Cover and cook
for the time specified, stirring once. Leave to stand, covered, for 2–3
minutes before serving.

Quantity	Water	Power	Minutes
450g/1lb	3 tbsp	100% (High)	8–10

FROZEN SLICED: Place in a cooking dish with the water. Cover and cook
for the time specified, stirring once. Leave to stand, covered, for 2–3
minutes before serving.

Quantity	Water	Power	Minutes
225g/8oz	2 tbsp	100% (High)	6
450g/1lb	3 tbsp	100% (High)	11–12

Lemons

TO GAIN MAXIMUM YIELD WHEN SQUEEZING: Prick the skins of the fruit and cook each for the time specified.

Quantity	Power	Seconds
1	100% (High)	5–10

Lentils

TO COOK: Place in a large dish with a little chopped onion, celery and lemon juice. Cover with boiling water or stock and add salt and pepper to taste. Cover and cook for the time specified, stirring once. Time cooking according to end use (if you need soft lentils for soup or a dip, use the longer cooking time; if you want them to retain some bite – say in a salad – use the shorter time).

Quantity	Water	Power	Minutes
225g/8oz	900ml/1½ pints	100% (High)	20–25

Liver

TO COOK FRESH LAMB'S LIVER: Preheat a browning dish according to the manufacturer's instructions: about 5 minutes. Add oil and butter. Add sliced, washed and dried liver, pressing down well. Cook for the first time specified. Turn over and cook for the second time specified, stirring or rearranging once.

Quantity	Oil	Butter	Power	1st Time	2nd Time
450g/1lb	1 tbsp	15g/½ oz	100% (High)	1 minute	4–5 minutes

FROZEN SLICES: Spread on a plate. Cover and cook for the time specified, turning twice. Leave to stand, covered, for 5 minutes before using.

Quantity	Power	Minutes
225g/8oz	20% (Defrost)	4–5
450g/1lb	20% (Defrost)	8–9

See also Chicken Livers (page 40)

Lobster

TO REHEAT COOKED WHOLE LOBSTER AND LOBSTER TAILS: Place in a cooking dish and cover with vented cling film. Cook for the time specified, turning over once. Leave to stand for 5 minutes before serving or using.

Quantity	Power	Minutes
450g/1lb whole	100% (High)	6–8
450g/1lb tails	100% (High)	5–6

TO THAW WHOLE COOKED FROZEN: Place in a cooking dish. Cover and cook for the time and power specified, giving the dish a quarter turn every 2 minutes and turning over after 6 minutes. Leave to stand for 5 minutes.

Quantity	Power	Minutes
per 450g/1lb	20% (Defrost)	12–15

M

MACKEREL
MANGETOUT
MARROW
MAYONNAISE
MEATBALLS
MELON
MILK
MILLET
MINCED BEEF
MIXED VEGETABLES
MOUSSE
MUNG BEANS
MUSHROOMS
MUSSELS

Mackerel _____

TO COOK FRESH: Remove heads and clean and gut. Slash the skin in 2 to
3 places to prevent bursting. Shield the tail-end with a little foil if
preferred. Place in a dish or on a roasting rack, season with salt,
pepper and lemon juice as desired, and cover with greaseproof paper.
Cook for the calculated time according to weight, turning and
rearranging once. Leave to stand, covered, for 2–3 minutes before
serving.

Quantity	Power	Minutes
per 450g/1lb	100% (High)	3–4

FROZEN WHOLE MACKEREL: To thaw, place on a roasting rack or in a
shallow dish and cook for the calculated time according to weight,
turning over once. Leave to stand for 10 minutes before using.

Quantity	Power	Minutes
per 450g/1lb	20% (Defrost)	5–7

Mangetout _____

FRESH: Trim and place in a cooking dish with the water. Cover and
cook for the time specified, stirring once. Leave to stand, covered, for
2 minutes before serving.

Quantity	Water	Power	Minutes
100g/4oz	1 tbsp	100% (High)	3–4
225g/8oz	2 tbsp	100% (High)	4–5

FROZEN: Place in a cooking dish with water. Cover and cook for time
specified, stirring once.

Quantity	Water	Power	Minutes
1×200g/7oz packet	2 tbsp	100% (High)	3–4

Marrow

FRESH: Peel, remove seeds and cut into small neat dice. Place in a cooking dish without any water. Cover loosely and cook for the time specified, stirring once. Leave to stand, covered, for 2–3 minutes before serving.

Quantity	Power	Minutes
450g/1lb	100% (High)	7–10

FROZEN: To defrost only, place in a cooking dish, cover and cook for the time specified, stirring once. Drain and pat dry to use as required.

Quantity	Power	Minutes
225g/8oz	20% (Defrost)	4–5
450g/1lb	20% (Defrost)	9–10

Mayonnaise

Beat the egg yolks (at room temperature) with a little salt, mustard powder, cayenne pepper and the lemon juice or wine vinegar. Place the oil in a jug and cook for the time specified. Slowly whisk the oil, drop by drop, into the egg mixture until it starts to thicken, then add in a thin steady stream.

Alternatively, place egg mixture in a blender and, with the motor running, add the oil in a thin steady stream and blend until thick and glossy.

Egg Yolks	Oil	Lemon Juice/Vinegar	Power	Seconds
3	300ml/½ pint	5 tsp	100% (High)	30

Meatballs

TO COOK BASIC MIXTURE: Make up basic mixture using 450g/1lb minced beef, 1 finely chopped onion, 6 tablespoons fresh bread-crumbs, 1 beaten egg and seasoning to taste. Shape into about 12 large or 20 small meatballs. Place, in a ring pattern if possible, in a shallow cooking dish. Cook for the time specified, rotating the dish and turning the meatballs over twice. Allow to stand for 2 minutes before serving. If cooking in a sauce (about 300ml/½ pint) add halfway through the cooking time, cover and cook for the remaining time.

Quantity	Power	Minutes
12 large or 20 small using 450g/1lb basic beef mixture	100% (High)	6–8

Melon

FROZEN IN SYRUP: Place in a dish, cover and cook for the time specified, separating the fruit as it thaws. Leave to stand, covered, for 5–10 minutes before serving.

Quantity	Power	Minutes
225g/8oz	20% (Defrost)	6
450g/1lb	20% (Defrost)	12

Milk

TO HEAT: Place cold milk in a large jug and cook for the time specified.

Quantity	Power	Minutes
150ml/¼ pint	100% (High)	1–1½
300ml/½ pint	100% (High)	2–2½

Millet

MILLET GRAINS: Toast if liked. Place in a large cooking dish with boiling water and salt. Cover loosely with a lid or vented cling film and cook for first time and power setting. Reduce power setting and cook for second time and power setting, stirring twice. Leave to stand, covered, for 3–5 minutes before serving. Fluff with a fork to separate the grains to serve.

Quantity	Water	Salt	1st Time/Power	2nd Time/Power
225g/8oz	650ml/22fl oz	1 tsp	3 minutes/ 100% (High)	12 minutes/ 50% (Medium)

Minced Beef

CANNED: Place in a cooking dish. Cover and cook at the power and time specified, stirring once.

Quantity	Power	Minutes
425g/15oz can	100% (High)	4

Mixed Vegetables

FROZEN: Place in a cooking dish with the water. Cover and cook for the time specified, stirring once. Leave to stand, covered, for 2 minutes before serving.

Quantity	Water	Power	Minutes
225g/8oz packet	2 tbsp	100% (High)	4–5
450g/1lb packet	2 tbsp	100% (High)	7–8

CANNED: Place in a cooking dish, cover and cook for the time and power specified, stirring once.

Quantity	Power	Minutes
142g/5oz can	100% (High)	1
298g/10½oz can	100% (High)	2

Mousse

FROZEN: Unwrap or remove lid and cook for the time specified, checking constantly. Leave to stand for 2–5 minutes before serving.

Quantity	Power	Minutes
Family block size	20% (Defrost)	1
Individual tub	20% (Defrost)	½

Mung Beans

TO COOK SOAKED BEANS: Place soaked beans in a cooking dish. Cover with boiling water. Cover and cook for the first time and power specified. Reduce the power setting and cook for the second time specified, adding extra boiling water to cover if needed. Drain to use as required.

Quantity	1st Time/Power	2nd Time/Power
225g/8oz	10 minutes/ 100% (High)	10–15 minutes/ 50% (Medium)

Mushrooms

FRESH WHOLE: Trim and wipe mushrooms. Place in a cooking dish with water or butter. Cover and cook for the specified time, stirring twice. Leave to stand for 1–2 minutes before serving. Season to taste after cooking.

Quantity	Butter	or Water	Power	Minutes
225g/8oz	25g/1oz	2 tbsp	100% (High)	3–4
450g/1lb	40g/1½oz	3 tbsp	100% (High)	4–5

FRESH SLICED: Trim, wipe and slice mushrooms. Place in a cooking dish with water or butter. Cover and cook for the specified time, stirring once. Leave to stand for 1–2 minutes before serving. Season to taste after cooking.

Quantity	Butter	or Water	Power	Minutes
225g/8oz	25g/1oz	2 tbsp	100% (High)	2–3
450g/1lb	40g/1½oz	3 tbsp	100% (High)	3–4

FROZEN WHOLE BUTTON: To thaw and cook, place in a shallow dish with a knob of butter. Cover and cook for the time specified, stirring twice. Season to taste to serve.

Quantity	Power	Minutes
100g/4oz	100% (High)	3–4
225g/8oz	100% (High)	5–6

CANNED: Place in a cooking dish, cover and cook for the power and time specified, stirring once.

Quantity	Power	Minutes
300g/10½oz can whole	100% (High)	2
213g/7½oz can sliced	100% (High)	1½
300g/10½oz can sliced	100% (High)	2

Mussels

FRESH: Scrub or brush and scrape, wash thoroughly and place in a large cooking dish with the water (or white wine if preferred). Cover loosely and cook for the time specified, stirring once. Remove with a slotted spoon, discarding any mussels that do not open.

Quantity	Water	Power	Minutes
675g/1½lb	75ml/3fl oz	100% (High)	5

TO THAW COOKED FROZEN SHELLED: Spread the mussels on a plate in a single layer. Cook for the power and time specified, stirring to rearrange once. Leave to stand for 2 minutes.

Quantity	Power	Minutes
225g/8oz	20% (Defrost)	3½–4

N

NECTARINES

Nectarines

TO PEEL FRESH: Place water in a bowl and cook for the time specified. Add the nectarines and leave to stand for 1–2½ minutes to loosen the skins. Remove with a slotted spoon and immerse in cold water – the skin will now peel away easily.

Quantity	Water	Power	Minutes
3–4	750ml/1¼ pints	100% (High)	9–10

TO PURÉE FRESH: Halve, stone, slice but do not peel nectarines. Place in a cooking dish, cover loosely and cook for the time specified, stirring once. Leave to stand, covered, for 3 minutes then purée in a blender or pass through a fine nylon sieve.

Quantity	Power	Minutes
450g/1lb	100% (High)	4–5
(to make 300ml/½ pint purée)		

POACHED IN LIGHT SYRUP: Skin and prick thoroughly. Place in a cooking dish with 300ml/½ pint hot sugar syrup and a dash of lemon juice. Cover loosely and cook for the time specified, stirring once. Leave to stand, covered, for 5 minutes. Serve hot or cold.

Quantity	Power	Minutes
8	100% (High)	6

TO STEW SLICES: Stone, wash and slice. Place in a dish with the sugar. Cover and cook for the time specified, stirring once. Leave to stand, covered, for 5 minutes before serving.

Quantity	Sugar	Power	Minutes
4 medium	100g/4oz	100% (High)	4–5

FROZEN HALVES IN SYRUP: Place in a dish, cover and cook for time specified, breaking up after half the time. Leave to stand, covered, for 10 minutes before using.

Quantity	Power	Minutes
225g/8oz	20% (Defrost)	10–12
450g/1lb	20% (Defrost)	13–15

FROZEN SLICES IN SYRUP: Place in a dish, cover and cook for the time specified, stirring once. Leave to stand, covered, for 5 minutes before using.

Quantity	Power	Minutes
225g/8oz	20% (Defrost)	6–7
450g/1lb	20% (Defrost)	12–13

O

OATS
OKRA
ONIONS
ORANGE JUICE
ORANGES

Oats

OAT GRAINS: Toast if preferred. Place in a large cooking dish with boiling water and salt. Cover loosely with a lid or vented cling film and cook for first time and power setting. Reduce power setting and cook for second time specified, stirring twice. Leave to stand, covered, for 5–10 minutes before serving. Fluff the grains with a fork to separate to serve.

Quantity	Water	Salt	1st Time/Power	2nd Time/Power
175g/6oz	750ml/1¼ pints	1 tsp	3 minutes/ 100% (High)	20–22 minutes/ 50% (Medium)

Okra

FRESH: Top and tail and sprinkle lightly with salt. Leave to drain for 30 minutes. Rinse and place in a cooking dish with the water or butter. Cover and cook for the time specified, stirring once. Leave to stand, covered, for 3 minutes before serving.

Quantity	Water	or	Butter	Power	Minutes
450g/1lb	2 tbsp		25g/1oz	100% (High)	8–10

Onions

FRESH WHOLE: Peel and place in a cooking dish. Cover and cook for the specified time, rearranging and rotating once. Leave to stand, covered, for 2 minutes before serving.

Quantity	Power	Minutes
450g/1lb or 4 medium	100% (High)	10–12

FRESH SLICED: Peel and cut into thin wedges or slices. Place in a cooking dish with the butter and water. Cover loosely and cook for the specified time, stirring once. Leave to stand, covered, for 5 minutes before serving.

Quantity	Butter	Water	Power	Minutes
450g/1lb	25g/1oz	2 tbsp	100% (High)	7–10

FROZEN WHOLE: Place in a cooking dish with the water. Cover and cook for the time specified, stirring once. Leave to stand, covered, for 2–3 minutes before serving.

Quantity	Water	Power	Minutes
100g/4oz packet small whole	6 tbsp	100% (High)	2–3

FROZEN SLICES OR RINGS: Place in a shallow dish, cover and cook for the time specified, stirring twice. Drain to use.

Quantity	Power	Minutes
225g/8oz	20% (Defrost)	4–5
450g/1lb	20% (Defrost)	8

Orange Juice

FROZEN CONCENTRATED: To thaw, remove lid and place in a jug. Cook for time specified, stirring once. Add cold water to dilute to serve.

Quantity	Power	Minutes
1×178ml/6¼ fl oz	100% (High)	1–1½

Oranges

POACHED IN LIGHT SYRUP: Peel if preferred, or scrub the skin, then finely slice. Place in a cooking dish with 300ml/½ pint hot sugar-syrup. Cover loosely and cook for the time specified, stirring once. Leave to stand, covered, for 5 minutes. Serve hot or cold.

Quantity	Power	Minutes
4	100% (High)	3

P

PAK SOI (OR BOK CHOY CABBAGE)
PARSLEY SAUCE
PARSNIPS
PASTA
PASTRY
PÂTÉ
PEACHES
PEANUTS
PEARS
PEAS
PEPPERS
PIMIENTOS
PINEAPPLE
PINTO BEANS
PIZZA
PLAICE
PLATED MEALS
PLUMS
POPPADUMS
PORK
PORRIDGE
POTATOES
POT ROAST
POUSSINS
PRAWNS AND SHRIMPS
PROVING DOUGH
PUMPKIN

Pak Soi (or Bok Choy Cabbage) ———————————

FRESH: Slice stalks and leaves and place in a large dish so that the cabbage fits loosely. Add water, cover and cook for the time specified, stirring once. Leave to stand for 3–5 minutes before serving. Season after cooking.

Quantity	Water	Power	Minutes
450g/1lb	2 tbsp	100% (High)	6–8

Parsley Sauce ————————————————————

TO MAKE BASIC POURING OR COATING SAUCE: Follow the instructions for white sauce on page 152. Add 1 tablespoon chopped fresh parsley for the last 2 minutes cooking time.

FROZEN: To thaw and reheat. Place in a cooking dish, cover and cook for the time specified, stirring twice. Whisk to serve.

Quantity	Power	Minutes
300ml/½ pint	100% (High)	4–5

Parsnips ———————————————————————

FRESH WHOLE: Peel and prick with a fork. Arrange in a large shallow dish, with tapered ends to centre. Dot with butter and add water and lemon juice. Cover and cook for the time specified, rearranging once. Leave to stand, covered, for 3 minutes before serving.

Quantity	Butter	Water	Lemon Juice	Power	Minutes
450g/1lb	15g/½oz	3 tbsp	1 tbsp	100% (High)	9–12

FRESH SLICES: Peel and slice. Place in a cooking dish with the butter and add water and lemon juice. Cover and cook for the time specified, stirring twice. Leave to stand, covered, for 3 minutes before serving.

Quantity	Butter	Water	Lemon Juice	Power	Minutes
450g/1lb	15g/½oz	3 tbsp	1 tbsp	100% (High)	9–12

FRESH CUBES: Peel and cut into 1.5cm/½ inch cubes. Place in a cooking dish with the butter and add water and lemon juice. Cover and cook for the time specified, stirring twice. Leave to stand, covered, for 3 minutes before serving.

Quantity	Butter	Water	Lemon Juice	Power	Minutes
450g/1lb	15g/½oz	3 tbsp	1 tbsp	100% (High)	9–12

FROZEN WHOLE: To thaw and cook. Arrange in a shallow dish, with tapered ends to centre. Cover and cook for the time specified, rearranging once. Toss in butter and seasoning to taste to serve.

Quantity	Power	Minutes
225g/8oz	100% (High)	7–8
450g/1lb	100% (High)	9–10

FROZEN SLICES: To thaw and cook. Place in a cooking dish, cover and cook for the time specified, stirring twice. Toss in butter and seasoning to taste to serve.

Quantity	Power	Minutes
225g/8oz	100% (High)	6–7
450g/1lb	100% (High)	12–14

FROZEN CUBES: To thaw and cook. Place in a cooking dish, cover and cook for the time specified, stirring twice. Toss in butter and seasoning to taste to serve.

Quantity	Power	Minutes
225g/8oz	100% (High)	4–5
450g/1lb	100% (High)	7–9

Pasta

PRE-COOKING LASAGNE FOR LAYERING WITH MEAT MIXTURE: Place lasagne in a large rectangular dish with the boiling water and a pinch of salt. Cover and cook for the time specified, rearranging the sheets once. Drain and rinse under cold running water to use.

Quantity	Water	Power	Minutes
225g/8oz	750ml/1¼ pints	100% (High)	7–9

PRE-COOKING CANNELLONI FOR STUFFING: Place the cannelloni in a dish and add the boiling water and a pinch of salt. Cover and cook for the time specified. Leave to stand for 5 minutes then drain and stuff and cover with chosen sauce.

Quantity	Water	Power	Minutes
225g/8oz	750ml/1¼ pints	100% (High)	1

FRESH PASTA (all types): Place pasta in a large dish with a little oil and the boiling water. Cover and cook for the time specified. Drain and use as required.

Quantity	Boiling Water	Power	Minutes
225g/8oz	750ml/1¼ pints	100% (High)	2–3

CANNED PASTA: Place canned pasta (macaroni cheese, ravioli in tomato sauce, spaghetti in tomato sauce or pasta shapes in sauce, for example) in a bowl, cover and cook for the time specified, stirring once.

Quantity	Power	Minutes
1×213g/7½oz can	100% (High)	1½–2
1×397g/14oz can	100% (High)	2½–3
1×425g/15oz can	100% (High)	2½–3

DRIED PASTA: Place the pasta in a large bowl with the boiling water and a little oil. Cook for the time specified, stirring once. Leave to stand for 3–5 minutes before draining to serve.

Quantity	Water	Power	Minutes
225g/8oz egg noodles and tagliatelle	1.2 litres/2 pints	100% (High)	6
225g/8oz short-cut macaroni	1.2 litres/2 pints	100% (High)	10
225g/8oz pasta shells and shapes	1.2 litres/2 pints	100% (High)	12–14
225g/8oz spaghetti	1.2 litres/2 pints	100% (High)	10–12
225g/8oz ravioli	1.5 litres/2½ pints	100% (High)	10

FROZEN COOKED PASTA: To thaw and reheat, place in a dish, cover and cook for the time specified, stirring twice.

Quantity	Power	Minutes
275g/10oz	20% (Defrost)	10

Pastry

FROZEN SHORTCRUST AND PUFF: Do not remove from wrappings unless unsuitable for the microwave. Cook for time specified and leave to stand for 5 minutes before using.

Quantity	Power	Minutes
1×210g/7½oz pkt	20% (Defrost)	2½–3
1×370g/13oz pkt	20% (Defrost)	4

Pâté

FROZEN PÂTÉ: Unwrap and place on a plate or leave in dish if suitable for microwave. Cover and cook for the time specified, rotating 2–3 times. Leave to stand for 15–20 minutes before serving.

Quantity	Power	Minutes
1×115g/4½oz pack	20% (Defrost)	1
1×198g/7oz pack	20% (Defrost)	3–4
1×275g/10oz slice	20% (Defrost)	3–4

Peaches

TO PEEL FRESH: Place water in a bowl and cook for the time specified. Add the peaches and leave to stand for 1–2½ minutes to loosen the skins. Remove with a slotted spoon and immerse in cold water – the skins will now peel away easily.

Quantity	Water	Power	Minutes
3–4	750ml/1¼ pints	100% (High)	9–10

TO PURÉE FRESH: Halve, stone, slice but do not peel the peaches. Place in a cooking dish, cover loosely and cook for the time specified, stirring once. Leave to stand, covered, for 3 minutes then purée in a blender or pass through a fine nylon sieve.

Quantity	Power	Minutes
450g/1lb (to make 300ml/½ pint purée)	100% (High)	4–5

POACHED IN LIGHT SYRUP: Skin, stone and slice, or skin and prick thoroughly but leave whole. Place in a cooking dish with 300ml/ ½ pint hot sugar syrup. Cover loosely and cook for the time specified, stirring once. Leave to stand, covered, for 5 minutes. Serve hot or cold.

Quantity	Power	Minutes
4 whole	100% (High)	4
4 sliced	100% (High)	3

TO STEW SLICES: Stone, wash and slice. Place in a dish with the sugar. Cover and cook for the time specified, stirring once. Leave to stand, covered, for 5 minutes before serving.

Quantity	Sugar	Power	Minutes
4 medium	100g/4oz	100% (High)	4–5

FROZEN HALVES IN SYRUP: Place in a dish, cover and cook for time specified, breaking up after half the time. Leave to stand, covered, for 10 minutes before using.

Quantity	Power	Minutes
225g/8oz	20% (Defrost)	10–12
450g/1lb	20% (Defrost)	13–15

FROZEN SLICES IN SYRUP: Place in a dish, cover and cook for the time specified, stirring once. Leave to stand, covered, for 5 minutes before using.

Quantity	Power	Minutes
225g/8oz	20% (Defrost)	6–7
450g/1lb	20% (Defrost)	12–13

Peanuts

TO ROAST: Place shelled, husked raw nuts on a large shallow plate. Add the oil and toss to coat. Cook for the time specified, stirring and turning twice. Allow to cool on absorbent kitchen towel. Season with salt if preferred.

Quantity	Oil	Power	Minutes
150g/5oz	1 tsp	100% (High)	5–7

Pears

POACHED IN LIGHT SYRUP: Peel and prick if kept whole, or halve and core. Place in a cooking dish with 300ml/½ pint sugar syrup. Cover loosely and cook for the time specified, stirring once. Leave to stand, covered, for 5 minutes. Serve hot or cold.

Quantity	Power	Minutes
900g/2lb whole dessert	100% (High)	5
900g/2lb whole cooking	100% (High)	10
900g/2lb halved dessert	100% (High)	3

STEWED: Peel, halve and core. Dissolve the sugar in a little water and pour over the pears. Cover loosely and cook for the time specified, stirring once. Leave to stand, covered, for 5 minutes before serving.

Quantity	Sugar	Power	Minutes
6 medium	75g/3oz	100% (High)	8–10

FROZEN HALVES IN SYRUP: Place in a cooking dish, cover and cook for the time specified, separating pears at the end of the cooking time. Leave to stand, covered, for 5–10 minutes before using.

Quantity	Power	Minutes
225g/8oz	20% (Defrost)	11–13
450g/1lb	20% (Defrost)	18–20

Peas

FRESH: Place in a cooking dish with butter and water. Cover and cook for the time specified, stirring once. Leave to stand, covered, for 3–5 minutes before serving.

Quantity	Butter	Water	Power	Minutes
100g/4oz	15g/½oz	2 tsp	100% (High)	3
225g/8oz	25g/1oz	1 tbsp	100% (High)	4–5
450g/1lb	50g/2oz	2 tbsp	100% (High)	6–8

FROZEN: Place in a cooking dish with water. Cover and cook for time specified, stirring once. Leave to stand, covered, for 3 minutes before serving.

Quantity	Water	Power	Minutes
1×225g/8oz packet	2 tbsp	100% (High)	4–6
1×450g/1lb packet	4 tbsp	100% (High)	6–8

CANNED: Drain all but liquid specified. Place in a cooking dish with liquid. Cover and cook for time specified, stirring once.

Quantity	Liquid	Power	Minutes
1×283g/10oz can	1½ tbsp	100% (High)	1–2
1×425g/15oz can	2 tbsp	100% (High)	2–3

See also Mangetout (page 89)

Peppers

TO BLANCH BEFORE STUFFING: Halve the peppers lengthways if preferred, or slice off tops to keep whole, and remove and discard the seeds. Place in a shallow dish with the water, cover and cook for the time specified, rotating the dish once. Drain to use.

Quantity	Water	Power	Minutes
4 halves or 2 whole	2 tbsp	100% (High)	6–8

TO COOK RINGS OR SLICES FOR HOT SALADS, RICE MIXTURES, ETC: Core, seed and slice the peppers. Place in a dish with the water, cover and cook for the time specified, stirring once. Leave to stand, covered, for 5 minutes before using.

Quantity	Water	Power	Minutes
4	1 tbsp	100% (High)	5–7

FROZEN: Place diced or sliced peppers in a bowl. Cover and cook for the time specified, stirring twice. Drain to use.

Quantity	Power	Minutes
50g/2oz diced	20% (Defrost)	1–1½
50g/2oz sliced	20% (Defrost)	2
100g/4oz diced	20% (Defrost)	2–2½
100g/4oz sliced	20% (Defrost)	2½–3

FROZEN COOKED STUFFED: To thaw and reheat, stand upright on a serving dish. Cover and cook for the time specified, rearranging twice. Cover with foil and leave to stand for 5 minutes before serving.

Quantity	Power	Minutes
2 whole stuffed	100% (High)	5
4 whole stuffed	100% (High)	10

Pimientos

CANNED: Place the pimientos in a cooking dish with the thickest parts arranged to the outer edge of the dish. Cover and cook for the time and power specified, stirring once.

Quantity	Power	Minutes
200g/7oz can	100% (High)	1
400g/14oz can	100% (High)	2½–3

Pineapple

POACHED IN LIGHT SYRUP: Peel, core and cut into bite-sized pieces. Place in a cooking dish with 300ml/½ pint hot sugar-syrup. Cover loosely and cook for the time specified, stirring once. Leave to stand, covered, for 5 minutes. Serve hot or cold.

Quantity	Power	Minutes
900g/2lb	100% (High)	5

Pinto Beans

TO COOK SOAKED BEANS: Place soaked beans in a cooking dish. Cover with boiling water. Cover and cook for the first time and power specified. Reduce the power setting and cook for the second time specified, adding extra boiling water to cover if needed. Drain to use as required.

Quantity	1st Time/Power	2nd Time/Power
225g/8oz	10 minutes/ 100% (High)	10–15 minutes/ 50% (Medium)

Pizza

LARGE FAMILY OR INDIVIDUAL SIZE: Roll out prepared yeast dough to a 30cm/12 inch circle, or 3×13cm/5 inch circles, and place on a large plate, pizza browner or microwave tray and cook for first time specified. Turn over and cover with chosen sauce, filling and topping. Cook for the second time specified.

Quantity	Power	1st Time	2nd Time
1×30cm/12 inch	100% (High)	3 minutes	2–3 minutes
or			
3×13cm/5 inch	100% (High)	3 minutes	2–3 minutes

FROZEN LARGE FAMILY OR INDIVIDUAL: To thaw and cook, place on a plate and cook for the time specified, rotating the dish twice.

Quantity	Power	Minutes
1×30cm/12 inch	100% (High)	3–5
1×13cm/5 inch	100% (High)	1½–2

Plaice

BRAISED/POACHED PLAICE FILLETS: Place a few slices of carrot, celery, onion and lemon in a large shallow dish with a bay leaf and 50ml/2fl oz water. Cover loosely with vented cling film. Cook for the first time specified. Add the fish fillets with the thicker portions to the outer edge of the dish. Re-cover and cook for the second time specified, rearranging and rotating once. Leave to stand, covered, for 5 minutes before serving.

Quantity	Power	1st Time	2nd Time
550g/1¼lb	100% (High)	4–6 minutes	5–7½ minutes

STEAMED PLAICE FILLETS: Arrange the fish fillets in a large dish with the thicker portions to the outside of the dish. Dot with a little butter, sprinkle with lemon juice and season with pepper. Cover with vented cling film and cook for the time specified, rearranging once. Leave to stand, covered, for 3 minutes before serving.

Quantity	Power	Minutes
450g/1lb	100% (High)	4–6

FROZEN PLAICE FILLETS: To thaw, place in a dish with the thicker portions to the outer edge. Cover and cook for the time specified, rearranging once. Leave to stand for 5 minutes before using.

Quantity	Power	Minutes
450g/1lb	20% (Defrost)	7–8

FROZEN WHOLE PLAICE: To thaw, place on a plate. Cover and cook for the time specified, shielding the tail-end with a little foil half-way through cooking as necessary. Leave to stand for 5 minutes before using.

Quantity	Power	Minutes
1×275g/10oz	20% (Defrost)	4–6
2×275g/10oz	20% (Defrost)	10–12

Plated Meals

TO REHEAT: Cover chilled, prepared plated meal with vented cling film and cook for the time specified.

Quantity	Power	Minutes
1×plated meal (with 175g/6oz meat and 275g/10oz vegetables)	100% (High)	3–4

Plums

POACHED IN LIGHT SYRUP: Prick whole, or halve and stone. Place in a cooking dish with 300ml/½ pint hot sugar syrup. Cover loosely and cook for the time specified, stirring once. Leave to stand, covered, for 5 minutes. Serve hot or cold.

Quantity	Power	Minutes
450g/1lb whole	100% (High)	3
450g/1lb halved	100% (High)	2

STEWED: Stone and wash. Place in a cooking dish with the sugar and a little grated lemon rind if preferred. Cover and cook for the time specified, stirring once. Leave to stand, covered, for 3–5 minutes before serving.

Quantity	Sugar	Power	Minutes
450g/1lb	100g/4oz	100% (High)	4–5

FROZEN WHOLE: Place in a cooking dish. Cover and cook for the time specified, stirring once. Leave to stand, covered, for 10 minutes before using.

Quantity	Power	Minutes
225g/8oz	20% (Defrost)	5–6
450g/1lb	20% (Defrost)	8–9

FROZEN IN SYRUP: Place in a cooking dish. Cover and cook for time specified, separating the plums at the end of the cooking time. Leave to stand, covered, for 10 minutes before using.

Quantity	Power	Minutes
225g/8oz	20% (Defrost)	5–7
450g/1lb	20% (Defrost)	13–14

Poppadums

PLAIN AND SPICED: Arrange on the base of the cooker or on turntable so that they do not touch or overlap. Cook until puffy and bubbling. Leave to stand on a wire rack for 15 seconds to crisp.

Quantity	Power	Seconds
1	100% (High)	20–25
2–3	100% (High)	45–60

Pork

PORK CHOPS: Brush the chops with a browning agent if desired, and place in a shallow dish or on a roasting rack with thicker portions to the outer edge of the dish. Cook for the time specified, turning over once. Leave to stand for 5–10 minutes before serving.

Quantity	Power	Minutes
2×100–175g/4–6oz loin	100% (High)	4–5
4×100–175g/4–6oz loin	100% (High)	6–8
2×225g/8oz chump or sparerib	100% (High)	8–10
4×225g/8oz chump or sparerib	100% (High)	11–13
2×275–350g/10–12oz rib	100% (High)	10–12
4×275–350g/10–12oz rib	100% (High)	16–20

PORK CHOPS COOKED IN BROWNING DISH: Preheat a large browning dish according to the manufacturer's instructions: about 5 minutes at 100% (High). Add the pork chops so that the meatiest portions are to the outer edge of the dish. Cook for the time specified, turning over once. Leave to stand for 5 minutes before serving.

Quantity	Power	Minutes
2×100–175g/4–6oz loin	100% (High)	4–5
4×100–175g/4–6oz loin	100% (High)	6–8
2×225g/8oz chump or sparerib	100% (High)	8–10
4×225g/8oz chump or sparerib	100% (High)	11–13

PORK FILLET OR TENDERLOIN: Shield the narrow, thin ends of the fillet or tenderloin with a little foil as necessary. Place on a roasting rack in a dish. Cook for the first time and power specified. Reduce the power and cook for the second time specified, turning over once. Leave to stand, covered with foil, for 5–10 minutes before serving.

Quantity	1st Time/Power	2nd Time/Power
1×350g/12oz	3 minutes/ 100% (High)	10–15 minutes/ 50% (Medium)
per 450g/1lb	3 minutes/ 100% (High)	14–18 minutes/ 50% (Medium)

ROAST PORK: I have given times for both 50% and 100% power for cooking roast pork because I think it cooks better in a microwave on the lower power setting (and has a crisper skin). However, the time savings (as compared with conventional oven roasting) are quickly eroded. Pork can be cooked at 100% very well and quickly, so I have given both options.

Place joint, skin or fat-side down, on a roasting rack or on an upturned saucer in a dish. Calculate the cooking time according to the joint type and size (weighing after stuffing, if appropriate). Cook for the chosen time and power setting, turning over once. Cover with foil and leave to stand for 20 minutes before serving. Brown and crisp any crackling under a preheated hot grill if preferred.

Type Pork	Cooking Time per 450g/1lb at 100% (High)	or	Cooking Time per 450g/1lb at 50% (Medium)
Boned leg or loin joint	8–10 minutes		13–15 minutes
Leg or hand joint on bone	8–9 minutes		12–14 minutes

FROZEN PORK CHOPS: To thaw, place on a roasting rack and cook for the time specified, turning and rearranging once. Leave to stand for 10 minutes before using.

Quantity	Power	Minutes
2×100–175g/4–6oz loin	20% (Defrost)	3–4
4×100–175g/4–6oz loin	20% (Defrost)	6–8
2×225g/8oz chump or sparerib	20% (Defrost)	7–9
4×225g/8oz chump or sparerib	20% (Defrost)	14–16
2×275–350g/10–12oz rub	20% (Defrost)	8–12
4×275–350g/10–12oz rub	20% (Defrost)	16–18

FROZEN PORK FILLET OR TENDERLOIN: To thaw, place on a roasting rack and cook for the time specified, turning over once. Leave to stand for 10 minutes before using.

Quantity	Power	Minutes
1×350g/12oz	20% (Defrost)	3–4
per 450g/1lb	20% (Defrost)	5–6

FROZEN UNCOOKED PORK JOINT: To thaw, place the joint on a roasting rack in a dish and cook for the time calculated below, turning over once. Leave to stand, covered, for 20–45 minutes before using.

Type Pork	Total Cooking Time (for calculation)	Power
Joints on bone	7–8 minutes per 450g/1lb	20% (Defrost)
Boneless joints	7–8 minutes per 450g/1lb	20% (Defrost)

See also Spareribs (page 135)

Porridge

TRADITIONAL OATMEAL: Place the oatmeal, salt and water or milk in a bowl, mixing well. Cover with vented cling film and cook for the time specified, stirring twice. Leave to stand, covered, for 2 minutes before serving.

Quantity	Salt	Water/Milk	Power	Minutes
30g/1¼oz (to serve 1)	¼ tsp	175ml/6fl oz	30% (Low)	10–12
65g/2½oz (to serve 2)	½ tsp	350ml/12fl oz	30% (Low)	10–12
125g/4½oz (to serve 4)	¾ tsp	750ml/1¼ pints	30% (Low)	12–14

QUICK-COOK OATMEAL: Place the oatmeal, salt and water or milk in a bowl, mixing well. Cover with vented cling film and cook for the time specified, stirring twice. Leave to stand, covered, for 2 minutes before serving.

Quantity	Salt	Water/Milk	Power	Minutes
30g/1¼oz (to serve 1)	¼ tsp	175ml/6fl oz	30% (Low)	5
65g/2½oz (to serve 2)	½ tsp	350ml/12fl oz	30% (Low)	5
125g/4½oz (to serve 4)	¾ tsp	750ml/1¼ pints	30% (Low)	7–8

Potatoes

MASHED OR CREAMED POTATOES: Peel potatoes, cut into 1.5cm/½ inch cubes and place in a cooking dish with the water. Cover and cook for time specified, stirring once. Leave to stand, covered, for 5 minutes. Drain and mash with butter and seasoning to taste.

Quantity	Water	Butter	Power	Minutes
900g/2lb	75ml/3fl oz	25g/1oz	100% (High)	11–13

NEW POTATOES OR OLD PEELED AND QUARTERED: Scrub new potatoes and scrape if preferred. Peel and quarter old potatoes. Place in a cooking dish with the water. Cover and cook for the time specified, stirring once. Leave to stand, covered, for 5 minutes before serving.

Quantity	Water	Power	Minutes
450g/1lb old	4 tbsp	100% (High)	7–10
450g/1lb new	4 tbsp	100% (High)	6–8

JACKET BAKED IN SKINS: Scrub and prick skin. Place on a double sheet of absorbent kitchen towel. Cook for the time specified, turning over once. If cooking more than 2 potatoes arrange in a ring pattern. Leave to stand for 3–4 minutes before serving.

Quantity	Power	Minutes
1×175g/6oz	100% (High)	4–6
2×175g/6oz	100% (High)	6–8
3×175g/6oz	100% (High)	8–12
4×175g/6oz	100% (High)	12–15

FROZEN NEW BOILED POTATOES: To thaw and reheat, place in a dish, cover and cook for the time specified, stirring twice. Leave to stand for 2 minutes before serving.

Quantity	Power	Minutes
225g/8oz	100% (High)	2½–3
450g/1lb	100% (High)	5–6

INSTANT MASHED POTATOES: Place milk and water in a bowl. Cook for the first time and power specified. Stir in the instant potato and cook for the second time and power specified or until all the liquid has been absorbed. Beat well before serving.

Milk and Water	Instant Potato	1st Time	2nd Time	Power
400ml/14fl oz	6 tbls	2–2½ minutes	3–4 minutes	100% (High)

TO COOK FROZEN OVEN CHIPS: Preheat a large browning dish according to the manufacturer's instructions, about 6 minutes at 100% (High). Brush lightly with oil and add the chips. Cook for the time and power specified, turning over halfway through the cooking time. Serve at once.

Quantity	Power	Minutes
175g/6oz	100% (High)	6–7
250g/12oz	100% (High)	11–12

TO COOK FROZEN POTATO CROQUETTES: Preheat a large browning dish according to the manufacturer's instructions, about 6 minutes at 100% (High). Brush lightly with oil and add the croquettes. Cook for the time and power specified, turning over once. Serve at once.

Quantity	Power	Minutes
4	100% (High)	4–5
8	100% (High)	7–8
16	100% (High)	14–15

TO COOK FROZEN POTATO WAFFLES: Preheat a large browning dish according to the manufacturer's instructions, about 6 minutes at 100% (High). Brush lightly with oil and add the waffles. Cook for the time and power specified, turning over once. Serve at once.

Quantity	Power	Minutes
1	100% (High)	4–5
2	100% (High)	5–6
4	100% (High)	6–7

TO COOK FROZEN POTATO SHAPES: Preheat a large browning dish according to the manufacturer's instructions, about 6 minutes at 100% (High). Brush lightly with oil and add the potato shapes. Cook for the time and power specified, turning over once. Serve at once.

Quantity	Power	Minutes
100g/4oz	100% (High)	4–5
225g/8oz	100% (High)	5–7
450g/1lb	100% (High)	9–11

CANNED: Place in a cooking dish, cover and cook for the power and time specified, stirring once.

Quantity	Power	Minutes
283g/10oz can	100% (High)	2
538g/1lb 3oz can	100% (High)	4

See also Sweet Potatoes (page 141)

Pot Roast

TO COOK TRADITIONAL STYLE: Place beef and stock or sauce in a large roasting or boiling bag. Secure and place in a dish. Cook for the first time and power specified, turn the beef over and cook for the second time and power specified, adding the vegetables after 20 minutes. Leave to stand, unopened, for 20–25 minutes before serving.

Quantity	Stock/Sauce	Vegetables	1st Time/Power	2nd Time/Power
1.5kg/3lb boneless rolled joint	150ml/¼ pint	450g/1lb prepared	8 minutes/ 100% (High)	45 minutes/ 50% (Medium)

Poussins

ROAST WHOLE: Rinse and dry then brush with a browning agent if preferred. Place on a roasting rack, breast-side down, cover loosely with greaseproof paper and cook for half the time specified. Rearrange and turn breast-side up, re-cover and cook for the remaining time. Allow to stand, covered, for 5 minutes before serving.

Quantity	Power	Minutes
1×450g/1lb	100% (High)	9–10
2×450g/1lb	100% (High)	20–22
4×450g/1lb	100% (High)	35–40

FROZEN WHOLE: To thaw, place on a plate or in a shallow dish, breast-side down, cover loosely and cook for half the recommended time. Turn breast-side up, rearrange (if more than one) and cook for the remaining time. Allow to stand, covered, for 5–10 minutes before using.

Quantity	Power	Minutes
1×450g/1lb	20% (Defrost)	6–7
2×450g/1lb	20% (Defrost)	12–14
4×450g/1lb	20% (Defrost)	24–28

Prawns and Shrimps

FRESH UNCOOKED: Place rinsed prawns in a dish with water, a bayleaf and dash of vinegar. Cover tightly with vented cling film. Cook for time specified, stirring once. Leave to stand, covered, for 3 minutes. Drain and cool quickly.

Quantity	Water	Power	Minutes
450g/1lb	600ml/1 pint	100% (High)	6–8
900g/2lb	600ml/1 pint	100% (High)	8–10

FROZEN COOKED: To thaw, place in a dish and cook for the time specified, stirring twice.

Quantity	Power	Minutes
450g/1lb	20% (Defrost)	7–8

Proving Dough

Bread dough proving can be hastened using the microwave. Simply give the dough a short burst of energy during the rising process, then leave to stand for 5–10 minutes before repeating until the dough has risen sufficiently. It is suggested that a burst of energy at 100% (High) power for 5–10 seconds is ideal for proving a 900g/2lb piece of dough.

Pumpkin

TO COOK FRESH: Remove the skin, seeds and membrane and cut into 2.5cm/1 inch cubes. Place in a cooking dish with the butter. Cover and cook for the time and power specified, stirring twice. Leave to stand for 3 minutes then season to serve plain or mashed with cream and herbs.

Quantity	Butter	Power	Minutes
450g/1lb	15g/½oz	100% (High)	4–6

R

RASPBERRIES
RATATOUILLE
RED KIDNEY BEANS
RED OR GREY MULLET
RED SNAPPER
REDCURRANTS
RHUBARB
RICE
RICE PUDDING
ROLY POLY
ROSE COCOA OR BORLOTTI BEANS
RYE

Raspberries

POACHED IN LIGHT SYRUP: Hull and rinse. Place in a cooking dish with 300ml/½ pint hot sugar-syrup. Cover loosely and cook for the time specified, stirring once. Leave to stand, covered, for 5 minutes. Serve hot or cold.

Quantity	Power	Minutes
450g/1lb	100% (High)	2

FROZEN: To thaw, place in a dish and cook for the time specified, stirring once to loosen and rearrange.

Quantity	Power	Minutes
225g/8oz	20% (Defrost)	3–4

Ratatouille

CANNED: Place in a cooking dish, cover and cook for the power and time specified, stirring three times.

Quantity	Power	Minutes
400g/14oz can	100% (High)	3

Red Kidney Beans (Dried)

TO COOK SOAKED BEANS: Place soaked beans in a cooking dish. Cover with boiling water. Cover and cook for the first time and power specified. Reduce the power setting and cook for the second time specified, adding extra boiling water to cover if needed. Drain to use as required.

Quantity	1st Time/Power	2nd Time/Power
225g/8oz	10 minutes/ 100% (High)	20–25 minutes/ 50% (Medium)

Red or Grey Mullet

FRESH WHOLE: Arrange the cleaned and gutted mullet in a shallow dish. Slash the skin in 2 to 3 places to prevent bursting and sprinkle with a little lemon juice if desired. Cover and cook for the time specified, rearranging the fish or turning the dish once. Leave to stand, covered, for 5 minutes before serving.

Quantity	Power	Minutes
2×200–250g/7–9oz	100% (High)	3–5
4×200–250g/7–9oz	100% (High)	7–9

FROZEN WHOLE: To thaw, place in a shallow dish and cook for the time specified, turning or rearranging twice. Leave to stand for 5 minutes before using.

Quantity	Power	Minutes
2×200–250g/7–9oz	20% (Defrost)	9–11
4×200–250g/7–9oz	20% (Defrost)	19–21

Red Snapper

TO COOK WHOLE FRESH: Season scaled and gutted fish inside and out and place or wrap in a buttered greaseproof paper 'parcel'. Place on a baking dish and cook for the time specified, rearranging once. Leave to stand, covered, for 5 minutes before serving with a sauce as desired.

Quantity	Power	Minutes
2×450–550g/1–1½lb	100% (High)	6–9

FROZEN WHOLE: To thaw individually (for best results), place in a shallow dish, cover and cook for the time specified, turning over once. Rinse in cold water then dry to use.

Quantity	Power	Minutes
1×450–550g/1–1½lb	50% (Medium)	2½–3½

Redcurrants

FRESH: Top and tail and place in a cooking dish with the sugar and water. Cover loosely and cook for the time specified, stirring once. Leave to stand for 5 minutes before serving.

Quantity	Sugar	Water	Power	Minutes
450g/1lb	100g/4oz	2 tbsp	100% (High)	5

FROZEN: Place in a cooking dish with the sugar and water. Cover loosely and cook for the time specified, stirring once. Leave to stand for 5 minutes before serving.

Quantity	Sugar	Water	Power	Minutes
450g/1lb	100g/4oz	2 tbsp	100% (High)	4–6

Rhubarb

FRESH: Cut into 2.5cm/1 inch lengths. Place in a cooking dish with the water. Cover loosely and cook for the time specified, stirring once. Stir in sugar and lemon juice. Leave to stand, covered, for 2–3 minutes.

Quantity	Water	Sugar	Lemon Juice	Power	Minutes
350g/12oz	2 tbsp	100g/4oz	1 tsp	100% (High)	6–7

POACHED IN LIGHT SYRUP: Cut into 2.5cm/1 inch lengths. Place in a cooking dish with 300ml/½ pint hot sugar syrup. Cover loosely and cook for the time specified, stirring once. Leave to stand, covered, for 5 minutes. Serve hot or cold.

Quantity	Power	Minutes
450g/1lb	100% (High)	4

FROZEN PIECES: Place in a cooking dish, cover and cook for the time specified, stirring once. Leave to stand, covered, for 5–10 minutes before using.

Quantity	Power	Minutes
225g/8oz	20% (Defrost)	5–6
450g/1lb	20% (Defrost)	8–9

Rice

LONG-GRAIN WHITE: Place in a large cooking dish with boiling water, salt and a knob of butter, if preferred. Cover loosely with a lid or vented cling film and cook for first time and power setting. Reduce power setting and cook for second time specified, stirring twice. Leave to stand, covered, for 5 minutes before serving. Fluff the rice with a fork to separate to serve.

Quantity	Water	Salt	1st Time/Power	2nd Time/Power
100g/4oz	300ml/½ pint	½ tsp	3 minutes/ 100% (High)	12 minutes/ 50% (Medium)
150g/5oz	350ml/12fl oz	½ tsp	3 minutes/ 100% (High)	12 minutes/ 50% (Medium)
175g/6oz	400ml/14fl oz	½ tsp	3 minutes/ 100% (High)	12 minutes/ 50% (Medium)
200g/7oz	475ml/16fl oz	¾ tsp	3 minutes/ 100% (High)	12 minutes/ 50% (Medium)
225g/8oz	550ml/18fl oz	1 tsp	3 minutes/ 100% (High)	12 minutes/ 50% (Medium)
275g/10oz	600ml/1 pint	1 tsp	3 minutes/ 100% (High)	12 minutes/ 50% (Medium)

LONG-GRAIN BROWN: Place in a large cooking dish with boiling water, salt and a knob of butter, if preferred. Cover loosely with a lid or vented cling film and cook for first time and power setting. Reduce power setting and cook for second time specified, stirring 2–3 times. Leave to stand, covered, for 5 minutes before serving. Fluff the rice with a fork to separate to serve.

Quantity	Water	Salt	1st Time/Power	2nd Time/Power
100g/4oz	300ml/½ pint	½ tsp	3 minutes/ 100% (High)	25 minutes/ 50% (Medium)
150g/5oz	350ml/12fl oz	½ tsp	3 minutes/ 100% (High)	25 minutes/ 50% (Medium)
175g/6oz	400ml/14fl oz	½ tsp	3 minutes/ 100% (High)	25 minutes/ 50% (Medium)
200g/7oz	475ml/16fl oz	¾ tsp	3 minutes/ 100% (High)	25 minutes/ 50% (Medium)
225g/8oz	550ml/18fl oz	1 tsp	3 minutes/ 100% (High)	25 minutes/ 50% (Medium)
275g/10oz	600ml/1 pint	1 tsp	3 minutes/ 100% (High)	25 minutes/ 50% (Medium)

LONG-GRAIN AND WILD RICE MIX: Place in a large cooking dish with boiling water, salt and a knob of butter. Cover loosely with a lid or vented cling film and cook for first time and power setting. Reduce power setting and cook for second time specified, stirring twice. Leave to stand, covered, for 5 minutes before serving. Fluff the rice mixture with a fork to separate to serve.

Quantity	Water	Salt	1st Time/Power	2nd Time/Power
1×400g/14oz packet	700ml/24fl oz	1 tsp	3 minutes/ 100% (High)	12 minutes/ 50% (Medium)

FROZEN COOKED RICE: To thaw and reheat, place in a dish, cover and cook for the time specified, stirring twice. Leave to stand, covered, for 2 minutes before using.

Quantity	Power	Minutes
225g/8oz	100% (High)	5–6
450g/1lb	100% (High)	7–8

See also Wild Rice (page 154)

Rice Pudding

TO COOK ROUND-GRAIN RICE PUDDING: Pour milk and evaporated milk into a large bowl. Add the rice, sugar and a pinch of spice if preferred. Cover and cook for first time and power specified, stirring 2–3 times. Reduce the power setting and cook for the second time specified, stirring twice. Leave to stand, covered, for 5 minutes before serving.

Milk	Evaporated Milk	Rice	Sugar	1st Time/Power	2nd Time/Power
250ml/ 8fl oz	1×170g/ 6oz can	5 tbsp	2 tbsp	6–8 minutes/ 100% (High)	30 minutes/ 50% (Medium)

TO COOK FLAKED RICE PUDDING: Pour milk into a large bowl and cook for first time and power specified. Add the rice, sugar, a knob of butter and a pinch of spice if preferred. Cover and cook for second time and power specified, stirring once. Leave to stand, covered, for 5 minutes before serving.

Milk	Rice	Sugar	1st Time/Power	2nd Time/Power
600ml/1 pint	5 tbsp	2 tbsp	6 minutes/ 100% (High)	15 minutes/ 50% (Medium)

Roly Poly

TO COOK: Roll out basic suet crust pastry (made with 175g/6oz self-raising flour, 75g/3oz shredded suet and 125ml/4fl oz water) to a rectangle 5mm/¼ inch thick. Spread with 5 tablespoons jam, syrup or marmalade. Roll up from short end, and place, seam-side down, on a lightly greased dish. Cook for time specified. Brown under a pre-heated hot grill if preferred.

Quantity	Power	Minutes
Made with 175g/6oz suet crust pastry (to serve 4)	100% (High)	4½–5

Rose Cocoa or Borlotti Beans (Dried)

TO COOK SOAKED BEANS: Place soaked beans in a cooking dish. Cover with boiling water. Cover and cook for the first time and power specified. Reduce the power setting and cook for the second time specified, adding extra boiling water to cover if needed. Drain to use as required.

Quantity	1st Time/Power	2nd Time/Power
225g/8oz	10 minutes/ 100% (High)	20–25 minutes/ 50% (Medium)

Rye

RYE GRAINS: Soak overnight or for 6–8 hours. Place in a large cooking dish with boiling water and salt. Cover loosely with a lid or vented cling film and cook for first time and power setting. Reduce power setting and cook for second time specified, stirring 3 times. Leave to stand, covered, for 5–10 minutes before serving. Fluff the grains with a fork to separate to serve.

Quantity	Water	Salt	1st Time/Power	2nd Time/Power
175g/6oz	750ml/1¼ pints	1 tsp	3 minutes/ 100% (High)	40 minutes/ 50% (Medium)

S

SALMON AND SALMON TROUT
SAUSAGEMEAT
SAUSAGES
SCALLOPS
SCAMPI
SCONES
SEMOLINA PUDDING
SHRIMPS
SMOKED HADDOCK
SMOKED SALMON
SOLE
SOUPS
SOYA BEANS
SPARERIBS
SPINACH
SPLIT PEAS
SPONGE PUDDING
SQUASH
STEAK AND KIDNEY PUDDING
STEAKS
STEW
STOCK
STRAWBERRIES
SUET PUDDING
SUGAR SYRUP
SWEDES
SWEET POTATOES
SWISS CHARD

Salmon and Salmon Trout _____

FRESH SALMON STEAKS: Arrange the salmon steaks in a shallow dish so that the tail-ends are to the centre of the dish. Brush with a little melted butter or sprinkle with a little lemon juice and herbs if desired. Cover with greaseproof paper and cook for the time specified, re-arranging or turning once. Leave to stand for 5 minutes before serving.

Quantity	Power	Minutes
2×225g/8oz	100% (High)	2–2½
4×225g/8oz	100% (High)	4–5
or 4×175g/6oz	50% (Medium)	9–10

TO COOK WHOLE SALMON OR SALMON TROUT: Prick the salmon skin in several places to prevent bursting and place in a shallow cooking dish. Add a little lemon juice and boiling water to moisten. Cover with greaseproof paper or vented cling film and cook for the time specified, rotating the dish 3 times. Leave to stand, covered, for 5 minutes before serving.

Quantity	Power	Minutes
1×450g/1lb	100% (High)	6–8
1×900g/2lb	100% (High)	10–14
1×1.5kg/3lb	100% (High)	15–19
1×1.8kg/4lb	100% (High)	20–22

FROZEN SALMON STEAKS: To thaw, place in a shallow dish, cover and cook for the time specified, turning over and rearranging once. Leave to stand, covered, for 5–10 minutes before using.

Quantity	Power	Minutes
2×225g/8oz	20% (Defrost)	4–5
4×225g/8oz	20% (Defrost)	10–12
4×175g/6oz	20% (Defrost)	10

FROZEN WHOLE SALMON OR SALMON TROUT: To thaw, place in a shallow dish, cover and cook for the time specified, turning over and rotating the dish twice. Shield the head and tail with a little foil as necessary. Leave to stand, covered, for 5–10 minutes before using.

Quantity	Power	Minutes
1×450g/1lb	20% (Defrost)	6–8
1×900g/2lb	20% (Defrost)	12–16
1×1.5kg/3lb	20% (Defrost)	18–20
1×1.8kg/4lb	20% (Defrost)	22–24

See also Smoked Salmon (page 133)

Sausagemeat

FROZEN: To thaw, remove any wrappings and place in a shallow dish. Cover and cook for the time specified, breaking up twice. Leave to stand, covered, for 4–5 minutes before using.

Quantity	Power	Minutes
450g/1lb	20% (Defrost)	6–8

Sausages

STANDARD SAUSAGES (50g/2oz each): Prick and place on a roasting rack in a cooking dish. Brush, if preferred, with a browning agent (soy sauce, Worcestershire sauce or proprietary mix, for example) and cover and cook for the first time specified. Turn sausages over, brush again with browning agent, cover and cook for second time specified.

Quantity	Power	1st Time	2nd Time
2	100% (High)	1½ minutes	1 minute
4	100% (High)	2 minutes	2 minutes
8	100% (High)	2½ minutes	2½ minutes

Alternatively, preheat a browning dish according to the manufacturer's instructions: about 5 minutes. Brush with a little oil and add the pricked sausages. Cover and cook for the first time specified above. Turn sausages over, cover and cook for the second time specified above.

CHIPOLATA SAUSAGES (25g/1oz each): Prick and place on a roasting rack in a cooking dish. Brush, if preferred, with a browning agent (soy sauce, Worcestershire sauce or proprietary mix, for example) and cover and cook for the first time specified. Turn chipolatas over, brush again with browning agent, cover and cook for the second time specified.

Quantity	Power	1st Time	2nd Time
2	100% (High)	¾ minute	½ minute
4	100% (High)	1 minute	¾ minute
8	100% (High)	1½ minutes	1 minute

Alternatively, preheat a browning dish according to the manufacturer's instructions: about 5 minutes. Brush with a little oil and add the pricked chipolatas. Cover and cook for the first time specified above. Turn chipolatas over, cover and cook for the second time specified above.

FROZEN: To thaw separated or linked sausages, place on a plate, cover and cook for the time specified, separating, turning over and rearranging twice. Leave to stand, covered, for 2–5 minutes before using.

Quantity	Power	Minutes
4 standard	20% (Defrost)	3–4
8 standard	20% (Defrost)	5–6
8 chipolatas	20% (Defrost)	3
16 chipolatas	20% (Defrost)	5

Scallops

FRESH: Place in a shallow dish. Cover with dampened absorbent kitchen towel and cook for the time specified, rearranging once. Leave to stand, covered, for 3 minutes before using or serving.

Quantity	Power	Minutes
450g/1lb	100% (High)	4–6
or 450g/1lb	50% (Medium)	8–12

FROZEN: Place in a bowl, cover and cook for the time specified, stirring and breaking apart twice. Leave to stand, covered, for 5 minutes before using.

Quantity	Power	Minutes
1×350g/12oz packet	20% (Defrost)	6–8
450g/1lb	20% (Defrost)	7½–10

Scampi ────────────────────────────────

FRESH UNCOOKED: Place rinsed, shelled scampi in a dish with water, a bayleaf and dash of vinegar. Cover with vented cling film. Cook for the time specified, stirring once. Leave to stand, covered, for 3 minutes. Drain and use quickly.

Quantity	Water	Power	Minutes
450g/1lb	600ml/1 pint	100% (High)	6–8
900g/2lb	600ml/1 pint	100% (High)	8–10

FROZEN COOKED: To thaw, place in a dish and cook for the time specified, stirring twice.

Quantity	Power	Minutes
450g/1lb	20% (Defrost)	7–8

Scones ────────────────────────────────

TO COOK IN A BROWNING DISH: Make up basic mixture in usual way using 225g/8oz plain flour, 1 tablespoon baking powder, pinch of salt, 50g/2oz butter, 1 tablespoon castor sugar and 150ml/¼ pint milk. Stamp out 8–10 rounds using a 5cm/2 inch cutter. Preheat a large browning dish according to the manufacturer's instructions: about 5 minutes. Lightly brush with oil. Add the scones and cook for the time specified, turning over once. Allow to cool on a wire rack.

Quantity	Power	Minutes
8–10	100% (High)	2½–3

FROZEN: To thaw, place scones on a double thickness sheet of absorbent kitchen towel. Cook for the time specified, rearranging once.

Quantity	Power	Minutes
2	20% (Defrost)	1¼–1½
4	20% (Defrost)	3

Semolina Pudding

TO COOK: Place custard powder, semolina, sugar, egg yolks and milk in a dish, mixing well. Cook for first time and power specified, stirring twice. Reduce power setting and cook for second time specified, stirring twice. Fold in 2 stiffly beaten egg whites to serve.

Custard Powder	Semolina	Sugar	Egg Yolks	Milk	1st Time/Power	2nd Time
4 tsp	25g/1oz	50g/2oz	2	600ml/ 1 pint	8 minutes/ 100% (High)	10 minutes 30% (Low)

Shrimps

See Prawns and Shrimps (page 118)

Smoked Haddock

STEAMED SMOKED HADDOCK FILLETS: Arrange the fish fillets in a large dish with the thicker portions to the outside of the dish. Dot with a little butter, sprinkle with a little lemon juice and season with salt and pepper if preferred. Cover with vented cling film and cook for the time specified, rearranging once. Leave to stand, covered, for 3 minutes before serving.

Quantity	Power	Minutes
450g/1lb	100% (High)	5–6

POACHED SMOKED HADDOCK FILLETS: Arrange the smoked haddock fillets in a large dish with the thicker portions to the outside of the dish. Season with pepper and lemon juice if preferred, and pour over water or milk. Cover with vented cling film and cook for the time specified, rearranging once. Leave to stand, covered, for 3 minutes before serving.

Quantity	Liquid	Power	Minutes
450g/1lb	8 tbsp	100% (High)	5–6

FROZEN SMOKED HADDOCK FILLETS: To thaw and cook, place the frozen cook-in-bag on a plate and snip a couple of vents in the bag. Cook for the time specified, turning over once.

Quantity	Power	Minutes
1×175g/6oz packet	100% (High)	5–6

Smoked Salmon

FROZEN: To thaw, unwrap salmon and separate slices. Arrange evenly on a plate and cook for the time specified, turning once.

Quantity	Power	Minutes
1×85–100g/3–4oz packet	20% (Defrost)	1½–2

Sole

BRAISED/POACHED SOLE FILLETS: Place a few slices of carrot, celery, onion and lemon in a large shallow dish with a bayleaf and 50ml/2fl oz water. Cover loosely with vented cling film. Cook for the first time specified. Add the fish fillets with the thicker portions to the outer edge of the dish. Re-cover and cook for the second time specified, rearranging and rotating once. Leave to stand, covered, for 5 minutes before serving.

Quantity	Power	1st Time	2nd Time
550g/1¼lb	100% (High)	4–6 minutes	5–7½ minutes

STEAMED SOLE FILLETS: Arrange the fish fillets in a large dish with the thicker portions to the outside of the dish. Dot with a little butter, sprinkle with lemon juice and season with pepper. Cover with vented cling film and cook for the time specified, rearranging once. Leave to stand, covered, for 3 minutes before serving.

Quantity	Power	Minutes
450g/1lb	100% (High)	4–6

FROZEN SOLE FILLETS: To thaw, place in a dish with thicker portions to the outer edge. Cover and cook for the time specified, rearranging once. Leave to stand for 5 minutes before using.

Quantity	Power	Minutes
450g/1lb	20% (Defrost)	7–8

Soups

FROZEN: To defrost and reheat, place in a bowl, cover and cook for the time specified, breaking up and stirring 2–3 times.

Quantity	Power	Minutes
300ml/½ pint	100% (High)	4–4½
600ml/1 pint	100% (High)	7–7½

READY-MADE OR CANNED: To reheat, place in a bowl and cook for the time specified, stirring once.

Quantity	Power	Minutes
200ml/7fl oz (1 portion)	100% (High)	2½–3
1×283g/10oz can	100% (High)	3–3½
600ml/1 pint	100% (High)	5–7

Soya Beans

TO COOK SOAKED BEANS: Place soaked beans in a cooking dish. Cover with boiling water. Cover and cook for the first time and power specified. Reduce the power setting and cook for the second time specified, adding extra boiling water to cover if needed. Drain and use as required.

Quantity	1st Time/Power	2nd Time/Power
225g/8oz	10 minutes/ 100% (High)	20–25 minutes/ 50% (Medium)

Spareribs

TO ROAST: Place the individual spareribs on a roasting rack, season to taste and brush with browning agent if preferred. Cover and cook for the first time and power specified. Turning ribs over, reduce the power, then cover and cook for the second time specified, turning over and rearranging twice.

Quantity	1st Time/Power	2nd Time/Power
1.1–1.4kg/2½–3lb	5 minutes/ 100% (High)	24–30 minutes/ 50% (Medium)

Spinach

FRESH: Chop or shred and rinse. Place in a dish without any additional water. Cover and cook for the specified time, stirring once. Leave to stand for 2 minutes before serving. Season to taste after cooking.

Quantity	Power	Minutes
450g/1lb	100% (High)	6–8

FROZEN: Place in a dish. Cover and cook for the specified time, stirring to break up twice during the cooking. Season to taste after cooking.

Quantity	Power	Minutes
1×275g/10oz packet	100% (High)	7–9

CANNED: Place in a cooking dish, cover and cook for the power and time specified, stirring twice.

Quantity	Power	Minutes
270g/9½oz can	100% (High)	2
400g/14oz can	100% (High)	3

Split Peas (Yellow and Green)

TO COOK SOAKED PEAS: Place soaked peas in a cooking dish. Cover with boiling water. Cover and cook for the time specified.

Quantity	Power	Minutes
225g/8oz	100% (High)	10

Sponge Pudding

Cream 175g/6oz butter with 175g/6oz sugar. Beat in 3 eggs, fold in 175g/6oz self-raising flour and 4 tablespoons milk. Place in a 1.2 litre/2 pint pudding basin or 900g/2lb loaf dish greased and lined with a few digestive biscuit crumbs. Cook for the time specified, turning the dish every 2–3 minutes. Leave to stand for 2 minutes before turning out to serve.

Quantity	Power	Minutes
3 egg mixture	70%	9
(to serve 4–6)	(Medium/High)	

Squash

TO COOK FRESH: Pierce whole squash with a knife several times. Microwave for the time and power specified or until the flesh pierces easily with a skewer. Leave to stand for 5 minutes. Halve, scoop out the seeds and fibres and discard. Serve fresh in chunks or mashed with butter.

Quantity	Power	Minutes
per 450g/1lb	100% (High)	3–5

Steak and Kidney Pudding

CANNED: Remove from the can and place on a plate. Cover with vented cling film and cook for the power and time specified. Leave to stand for 2 minutes before serving.

Quantity	Power	Minutes
1 individual canned	100% (High)	2½–2¾

Steaks

TO COOK WITHOUT A BROWNING DISH: Rinse and dry steaks then brush with a little browning agent (soy sauce or Worcestershire sauce, for example), if preferred. Place in a lightly greased or oiled dish and cook for the first time specified according to taste. Turn over and cook for the second time specified according to taste. Cover with foil and leave to stand for 3–5 minutes.

Quantity	Power		1st Time	2nd Time
2×225g/8oz	100%	Rare:	1½ minutes	2½ minutes
rump, sirloin	(High)	Medium Rare:	2–2½ minutes	3 minutes
or fillet steaks		Medium:	2½–3 minutes	3–3½ minutes
or 450g/1lb		Well Done:	3½ minutes	4–5 minutes
T-bone steak				
4×225g/8oz	100%	Rare:	3–3½ minutes	3½–4 minutes
rump, sirloin	(High)	Medium Rare:	3½–4 minutes	4–4½ minutes
or fillet steaks		Medium:	4½–5 minutes	4½–5 minutes
or 900g/2lb		Well Done:	5–6 minutes	6–7 minutes
T-bone steak				

TO COOK WITH A BROWNING DISH: Rinse and dry steaks and snip fatty edge to prevent curling, if necessary. Preheat a browning dish according to the manufacturer's instructions: about 5 minutes. Add 2 teaspoons oil to the dish and swirl to coat. Add steaks and press down well. Cook for the time specified, turning once. Leave to stand for 1–2 minutes before serving.

Quantity	Power	Minutes
2×225g/8oz rump,	100% (High)	Rare: 1¾
sirloin or fillet		Medium Rare: 2¼–2½
steaks *or* 450g/1lb		Medium: 3–3½
T-bone steak		Well Done: 4½–5
4×225g/8oz rump,	100% (High)	Rare: 2¾–3
sirloin or fillet		Medium Rare: 3½–4
steaks		Medium: 4½–5
or 900g/2lb		Well Done: 7–7½
T-bone steak		

FROZEN: Place the steaks on a plate. Cover and cook for the time specified, turning over once. Leave to stand, covered, for 5–10 minutes before using.

Quantity	Power	Minutes
1×175–225g/6–8oz	20% (Defrost)	4
4×100–175g/4–6oz	20% (Defrost)	4–6
2×225g/8oz	20% (Defrost)	6–8

Stew

CANNED: Place in a cooking dish, cover and cook for the time and power specified, stirring once.

Quantity	Power	Minutes
425g/15oz can	100% (High)	3–4

Stock

TO MAKE VEAL, LAMB OR BEEF STOCK: Place stock bones in a large bowl and cover with boiling water. Add a selection of flavouring vegetables, a bouquet garni and salt and pepper to taste. Cover and cook on 100% power for 40 minutes, checking the stock level every 10 minutes and topping up if necessary to keep bones just covered.

Strain and cool completely. Skim and store in the refrigerator for up to 48 hours, or freeze for up to 6 months.

TO MAKE A POULTRY OR GAME STOCK: Place carcass in a large bowl and cover with boiling water. Add a selection of flavouring vegetables, a bouquet garni and salt and pepper to taste. Cover and cook on 100% power for 20 minutes, checking the stock level every 5 minutes and topping up if necessary to keep carcass just covered.

Strain and cool completely. Skim and store in the refrigerator for up to 48 hours, or freeze for up to 6 months.

TO MAKE A FISH STOCK: Place bones, head, tail and fish trimmings in a large bowl and cover with boiling water. Add a selection of flavouring vegetables, a bouquet garni and salt and pepper to taste. Cover and cook on 100% power for 10 minutes, checking the stock level once and topping up if necessary to keep ingredients just covered.

Strain and cool completely. Skim and store for up to 24 hours in the refrigerator. Do not freeze fish stock.

FROZEN: Place in a jug or bowl, cook uncovered, for the time specified, stirring and breaking up 2–3 times.

Quantity	Power	Minutes
300ml/½ pint	100% (High)	2½–3
600ml/1 pint	100% (High)	5–6

TO MAKE VEGETABLE STOCK: Place chopped vegetables and peelings in a bowl with the boiling water, a bouquet garni and salt and pepper to taste. Cover and cook for the first time and power specified. Reduce the power and cook for the second time specified. Strain and use or cool completely. Store in the refrigerator for up to 24 hours, or freeze for up to 3 months.

Quantity Vegetables	Water	1st Time/Power	2nd Time/Power
350g/12oz	1.2 litres/ 2 pints	10 minutes/ 100% (High)	10–15 minutes/ 50% (Medium)

Strawberries

POACHED IN LIGHT SYRUP: Hull and rinse. Place in a cooking dish with 300ml/½ pint hot sugar syrup. Cover loosely and cook for the time specified, stirring once. Leave to stand, covered, for 5 minutes. Serve warm or cold.

Quantity	Power	Minutes
450g/1lb	100% (High)	2

FROZEN: To thaw, place in a dish, cover and cook for the time specified, stirring gently twice. Leave to stand for 5–10 minutes before using.

Quantity	Power	Minutes
225g/8oz	20% (Defrost)	4–5
450g/1lb	20% (Defrost)	6–7

Suet Pudding

Mix 100g/4oz self-raising flour with 50g/2oz shredded suet and 50g/2oz castor sugar. Using a fork, gradually add 1 teaspoon vanilla essence, 1 beaten egg and 100ml/4fl oz milk, to make a soft batter. Place 3 tablespoons jam or syrup in the base of a greased 1.2 litre/ 2 pint pudding basin. Carefully spoon over the suet mixture. Cover with vented cling film and cook for the time specified, rotating the dish twice. Leave to stand for 2 minutes before turning out to serve.

Quantity	Power	Minutes
As above	100% (High)	4½–5
(to serve 4–6)		

Sugar Syrup

For poaching fruits place sugar and water in a heatproof jug and cook for the time specified, stirring 3 times.

Yield	Water	Sugar	Power	Minutes
300ml/½ pint	300ml/½ pint	100g/4oz	100% (High)	4–5

Swedes

FRESH: Peel and cut into 1.5cm/½ inch cubes. Place in a cooking dish with the water and butter. Cover and cook for the time specified, stirring twice. Leave to stand, covered, for 4 minutes. Drain and season to serve or mash with butter, cream and seasonings if preferred.

Quantity	Butter	Water	Power	Minutes
450g/1lb	15g/½ oz	2 tbsp	100% (High)	10–12

FROZEN: To thaw and cook cubed swede. Place in a cooking dish, cover and cook for the time specified, stirring twice. Toss in butter and seasonings or mash with butter, cream and seasonings if preferred.

Quantity	Power	Minutes
225g/8oz	100% (High)	5–6
450g/1lb	100% (High)	8–10

Sweet Potatoes

TO COOK FRESH: If cooking whole, prick the skins and place on a sheet of absorbent kitchen towel. Cook for the time and power specified, turning twice. Allow to cool for handling and peel away the skins to serve. Alternatively, cut into cubes and place in a bowl with the water. Cover and cook for the time and power specified, stirring twice. Drain, and toss with butter and seasonings to taste, to serve.

Quantity	Water	Power	Minutes
450g/1lb whole	–	100% (High)	7–9
900g/2lb whole	–	100% (High)	11–13
450g/1lb cubed	3 tbls	100% (High)	6–8
900g/2lb	5 tbls	100% (High)	10–12

Swiss Chard

FRESH: Remove and discard the thick stalk and shred the leaves. Place in a large cooking dish with the water. Cover and cook for the specified time, stirring every 3 minutes. Leave to stand for 2 minutes before serving. Season to taste after cooking.

Quantity	Water	Power	Minutes
450g/1lb	150ml/¼ pint	100% (High)	5½–6½

T

TEA
TEA CAKES
TOMATOES
TROUT
TURKEY
TURNIPS

Tea

FRESH: Place the water in a large jug and cook for the time specified or until just boiling. Add the tea or tea bags, cover and leave to infuse until the desired strength of tea is obtained. Use as required.

Quantity	Tea/Tea Bags	Power	Minutes
750ml/1¼ pints	4 tsp or 3 bags	100% (High)	5–6

Tea Cakes

FROZEN: To thaw, place on a double thickness piece of absorbent kitchen towel and cook for the time specified, rearranging once. Serve while still warm.

Quantity	Power	Minutes
2	100% (High)	1
4	100% (High)	1–1½

Tomatoes

TO PEEL FRESH: Boil 750ml/1¼ pints water conventionally and place in a bowl. Add pricked tomatoes, cover and cook for the time specified. Remove with a slotted spoon and plunge into cold water – the skin will now peel away easily.

Quantity	Power	Minutes
Up to 450g/1lb	100% (High)	½

TO COOK WHOLE AND HALVES: Prick, whole and/or halve tomatoes, arrange in a circle on a plate, cut-side up. Dot with butter and season with salt and pepper to taste. Cook for the time specified according to size and ripeness.

Quantity	Power	Minutes
1 medium	100% (High)	½
4 medium	100% (High)	2–2½
4 large (beef)	100% (High)	3½–4

Trout

FRESH WHOLE: Arrange the cleaned and gutted trout in a shallow dish. Slash the skin in 2 to 3 places to prevent bursting and sprinkle with a little lemon juice if preferred. Cover and cook for the time specified, rearranging or turning the dish once. Leave to stand, covered, for 5 minutes before serving.

Quantity	Power	Minutes
2×225–275g/8–10oz	100% (High)	3–5
4×225–275g/8–10oz	100% (High)	7–9

FROZEN WHOLE: To thaw, place in a shallow dish and cook for the time specified, turning or rearranging twice. Leave to stand for 5 minutes before using.

Quantity	Power	Minutes
2×225–275g/8–10oz	20% (Defrost)	9–11
4×225–275g/8–10oz	20% (Defrost)	19–21

Turkey

TO ROAST WHOLE: Stuff if preferred and truss into an even shape. Weigh and calculate cooking time. Divide the cooking time into quarters and place the turkey, breast-side down, in a large shallow dish. Brush with browning agent or melted butter. Cook for one quarter of the time. Turn on to one side, brush again to baste and cook for a second quarter of the cooking time. Turn on to second side and brush again to baste. Cook for the third quarter of the cooking time. At this stage, if some areas begin to overcook, then shield with small strips of foil. Turn the turkey breast-side up and baste again. Cook for the remaining quarter of the total time. Cover with foil and leave to stand for time specified. Use as required.

Quantity	Power	Cooking Time	Standing Time
2.7kg/6lb	100% (High)	42 minutes	10 minutes
4kg/9lb	100% (High)	63 minutes	15 minutes
5.5kg/12lb	100% (High)	84 minutes	20 minutes
6.8kg/15lb	100% (High)	105 minutes	25 minutes

TO COOK FRESH OR DEFROSTED TURKEY ROAST: Remove outer wrapper, place in a shallow dish and cook for the first time specified. Remove the inner wrapper, turn the roast over, baste with a glaze if preferred, and cook for the second time specified. Cover with foil and leave to stand for 10 minutes before carving.

Quantity	Power	1st Time	2nd Time
1×576g/1¼lb	70% (Medium/High)	7 minutes	10 minutes

TO ROAST TURKEY DRUMSTICKS: Place drumsticks on a roasting rack, meaty sections downwards. Baste with a browning agent if desired. Cover and cook for first time and power specified. Reduce the power setting to 50% (Medium) and cook for the second time specified, turning once. Leave to stand, covered, for 5 minutes before serving.

Quantity	1st Time/Power	2nd Time/Power
2×350–400g/12–14oz drumsticks	5 minutes/ 100% (High)	13–15 minutes/ 50% (Medium)
4×350–400g/12–14oz drumsticks	8 minutes/ 100% (High)	25–31 minutes/ 50% (Medium)

TO ROAST TURKEY BREASTS: Beat out flat if preferred and place in a shallow dish. Baste with browning agent if desired. Cook for the time specified, turning over once. Leave to stand for 2–3 minutes before serving.

Quantity	Power	Minutes
2×100g/4oz breasts	50% (Medium)	4–5
2×225g/8oz breasts	50% (Medium)	8–10
4×100g/4oz breasts	50% (Medium)	8–10
4×225g/8oz breasts	50% (Medium)	16–18

FROZEN WHOLE: To defrost frozen turkey, place bird breast-side down in a shallow dish and cook for a quarter of the time. Turn breast-side up and cook for a further quarter of the time. Shield wing tips and legs with foil and turn turkey over. Cook for the remaining time.

Quantity	Power	Minutes
2.7kg/6lb	50% (Medium)	21–33
4kg/9lb	50% (Medium)	32–50
5.4kg/12lb	50% (Medium)	42–66
6.8kg/15lb	50% (Medium)	53–83

FROZEN UNCOOKED TURKEY ROAST: To thaw, do not remove outer and inner wrappings. Place on a plate and cook for the time specified, turning over once. Leave to stand, covered, for 20 minutes before using.

Quantity	Power	Minutes
1×576g/1¼lb	20% (Defrost)	12–14

FROZEN TURKEY PIECES: To thaw, place in a dish with the meatiest parts to the outer edge of the dish and cook for 5–7 minutes per 450g/1lb at 30% (Low), turning over and rearranging once. Leave to stand, covered, for 10 minutes before using.

Quantity	Power	Minutes
2×350–400g/12–14oz drumsticks	30% (Low)	12–16
4×350–400g/12–14oz drumsticks	30% (Low)	24–26
2×100g/4oz breasts	30% (Low)	3–4
2×225g/8oz breasts	30% (Low)	5–7
4×100g/4oz breasts	30% (Low)	5–7
4×225g/8oz breasts	30% (Low)	10–12

Turnips

FRESH WHOLE: Choose only small to medium turnips. Peel and prick with a fork. Arrange in a ring pattern in a large shallow dish. Dot with the butter and add the water. Cover and cook for the time specified, rearranging once. Leave to stand, covered, for 3 minutes before serving.

Quantity	Butter	Water	Power	Minutes
450g/1lb	15g/½oz	3 tbsp	100% (High)	14–16

FRESH SLICES: Peel and slice. Place in a cooking dish with the butter and water. Cover and cook for the time specified, stirring twice. Leave to stand, covered, for 3 minutes before serving.

Quantity	Butter	Water	Power	Minutes
450g/1lb	15g/½oz	3 tbsp	100% (High)	11–12

FRESH CUBES: Peel and cut into 1.5cm/½ inch cubes. Place in a cooking dish with the butter and water. Cover and cook for the time specified, stirring twice. Leave to stand, covered, for 3 minutes before serving.

Quantity	Butter	Water	Power	Minutes
450g/1lb	15g/½oz	3 tbsp	100% (High)	12–14

V

VEAL
VICTORIA SANDWICH

Veal

TO COOK VEAL LOIN CHOPS: Arrange in a large dish and brush with a little melted butter and browning agent if preferred. Cover with vented cling film and cook for the time specified, turning and re-arranging once. Allow to stand, covered, for 5 minutes before serving.

Quantity	Power	Minutes
2×150–175g/5–6oz	50% (Medium)	10–13
4×150–175g/5–6oz	50% (Medium)	15–19
6×150–175g/5–6oz	50% (Medium)	18–23

TO COOK BREADCRUMB-COATED VEAL STEAKS OR ESCALOPES: Coat veal steaks or escalopes in egg and breadcrumbs. Preheat a large browning dish according to the manufacturer's instructions: about 5 minutes. Add oil and butter and swirl to coat. Add veal in a single layer, cook for the first time specified, turn over and cook for second time specified. Leave to stand, covered, for 5 minutes before serving.

Quantity	Oil	Butter	Power	1st Time	2nd Time
4×100g/4oz steaks	1 tbsp	25g/1oz	100% (High)	2 minutes	4–6 minutes

VEAL ROAST: Place the veal roast, fat or barded-side down, on a roasting rack or on an upturned saucer in a dish. Calculate the cooking time at 8½–9 minutes per 450g/1lb at 100% (High) or 11–12 minutes per 450g/1lb at 50% (Medium), turning the joint over half-way through the cooking time. At the end of the cooking time cover with foil, shiny side in, and leave to stand for 20 minutes before carving.

Quantity	Power/Minutes	or	Power/Minutes
900g/2lb	100% (High)/17–18		50% (Medium)/22–24
1.5kg/3lb	100% (High)/25–27		50% (Medium)/33–36
1.75kg/4lb	100% (High)/34–36		50% (Medium)/44–48
2.25kg/5lb	100% (High)/43–45		50% (Medium)/55–60

FROZEN VEAL CHOPS: To thaw, arrange in a dish so that the thicker portions are to the outer edge. Cover and cook for the time specified, turning and rearranging twice. Leave to stand, covered, for 5–10 minutes before using.

Quantity	Power	Minutes
2	20% (Defrost)	5–6
4	20% (Defrost)	8–10
6	20% (Defrost)	12–15

FROZEN VEAL ROAST: To thaw, place in a dish and cook for the time specified, turning over twice. Shield any thinner areas with foil as they defrost. Calculate any sizes of joint not given below at 8–9 minutes per 450g/1lb at 20% (Defrost). Leave to stand, covered, for 10–20 minutes before using.

Quantity	Power	Minutes
900g/2lb	20% (Defrost)	16–18
1.5kg/3lb	20% (Defrost)	24–27
1.75kg/4lb	20% (Defrost)	32–36
2.25kg/5lb	20% (Defrost)	40–45

FROZEN STEWING VEAL: To thaw, place in a dish, cover and cook for the time specified, stirring twice. Leave to stand, covered, for 10 minutes before using.

Quantity	Power	Minutes
225g/8oz	20% (Defrost)	5–7
450g/1lb	20% (Defrost)	10–11

Victoria Sandwich

Line a 20cm/8 inch deep cake dish with cling film, or grease and line base with greaseproof paper. Cream 175g/6oz butter with 175g/6oz castor sugar. Gradually beat in 3 eggs and fold in 175g/6oz plain flour sifted with 2 teaspoons baking powder. Finally fold in 2 tablespoons hot water. Spoon into the dish and level the surface, cook for the time specified, giving the dish a half-turn every 2 minutes. Leave to stand for 5 minutes to finish cooking before turning out onto a rack to cool. Split and fill with jam and cream when cold, as desired.

Quantity	Power	Minutes
3 egg mixture as above	100% (High)	6½–7½

W

WHEAT
WHITE SAUCE
WHITEBAIT
WHITING
WILD RICE

Wheat

WHEAT GRAINS: Soak overnight, or for 6–8 hours. Place in a large cooking dish with boiling water and salt. Cover loosely with a lid or vented cling film and cook for first time and power setting. Reduce power setting and cook for second time specified, stirring 3 times. Leave to stand, covered, for 5–10 minutes before serving. Fluff the wheat grains with a fork to separate to serve.

Quantity	Water	Salt	1st Time/Power	2nd Time/Power
175g/6oz	1 litre/1¾ pints	1 tsp	3 minutes/ 100% (High)	40 minutes/ 50% (Medium)

See also Bulghur (Cracked Wheat) page 29.

White Sauce

TO MAKE BASIC WHITE POURING SAUCE: Place butter in a jug and cook for first time specified. Blend in flour and milk and cook for second time specified, stirring once every minute until smooth, boiling and thickened. Season to taste to serve.

Butter	Flour	Milk	Power	1st Time	2nd Time
25g/1oz	25g/1oz	300ml/½ pint	100% (High)	1 minute	3½–4 minutes

TO MAKE BASIC WHITE COATING SAUCE: Place butter in a jug and cook for first time specified. Blend in flour and milk and cook for second time specified, stirring once every minute until smooth, boiling and thickened. Season to taste to serve.

Butter	Flour	Milk	Power	1st Time	2nd Time
50g/2oz	50g/2oz	300ml/½ pint	100% (High)	1 minute	3½–4 minutes

FROZEN: To thaw and reheat. Place in a cooking dish, cover and cook for time specified, stirring twice. Whisk to serve.

Quantity	Power	Minutes
300ml/½ pint	100% (High)	4–5

Whitebait

FROZEN: To thaw, place in a dish, cover and cook for the time specified, breaking gently apart. Leave to stand for 10–15 minutes before using.

Quantity	Power	Minutes
225g/8oz	20% (Defrost)	5–7

Whiting

BRAISED/POACHED WHITING FILLETS: Place a few slices of carrot, celery, onion and lemon in a large shallow dish with a bayleaf and 50ml/2fl oz water. Cover loosely with vented cling film. Cook for the first time specified. Add the fish fillets with the thicker portions to the outer edge of the dish. Re-cover and cook for the second time specified, rearranging and rotating once. Leave to stand, covered, for 5 minutes before serving.

Quantity	Power	1st Time	2nd Time
550g/1¼lb	100% (High)	4–6 minutes	5–7½ minutes

STEAMED WHITING FILLETS: Arrange the fish fillets in a large dish with the thicker portions to the outside of the dish. Dot with a little butter, sprinkle with lemon juice and season with pepper. Cover with vented cling film and cook for the time specified, rearranging once. Leave to stand, covered, for 3 minutes before serving.

Quantity	Power	Minutes
450g/1lb	100% (High)	4–6

FROZEN WHITING FILLETS: To thaw, place in a dish with thicker portions to outer edge. Cover and cook for the time specified, re-arranging once. Leave to stand for 5 minutes before using.

Quantity	Power	Minutes
450g/1lb	20% (Defrost)	7–8

Wild Rice

Soak the rice in 600ml/1 pint warm water for 2–3 hours. Drain thoroughly. Place in a bowl with the oil, boiling water and seasonings to taste. Cover and cook for the time specified, stirring once. Leave to stand, covered, for 5 minutes before serving.

Quantity	Oil	Water	Power	Minutes
100g/4oz	1 tbsp	600ml/1 pint	100% (High)	30

Y

YOGHURT

Yoghurt

FROZEN: To thaw, remove lid and cook for the time specified. Stir well and leave to stand for 1–2 minutes before serving.

Quantity	Power	Minutes
1×142g/5oz carton	100% (High)	1

TO MAKE FRESH: Place the milk in a large jug and cook, uncovered, for the time specified (or until boiling). Cover and allow to cool until tepid – up to 30 minutes. Add the live natural yoghurt, blending well and pour into a warmed wide-necked flask. Seal and leave, undisturbed, to set – at least 8 hours.

Quantity Milk	Power	Minutes	Live Natural Yoghurt
600ml/1 pint	100% (High)	5–6	3 tbsp